BRITISH COMPENDIUM

◆

PHOTO MEMORIES OF 2,000 CITIES, TOWNS
& VILLAGES IN BRITAIN

THE FRANCIS FRITH COLLECTION

SHAFTESBURY DORSET

This edition published 1997 by
Universal Books Ltd, The Grange, Grange Yard,
London SE1 3AG

Text and introduction by Terence Sackett

© The Francis Frith Collection

ISBN 1 84013 096 2

Printed and bound by
WBC Book Manufacturers Ltd
Bridgend, Mid Glamorgan

The Francis Frith Collection
The Old Rectory, Bimport, Shaftesbury, Dorset SP7 8AT

Title Page Photograph: *24835 Northam Village, Devon 1890*

FRAMED & MOUNTED PRINTS

All the photographs pictured in this Compendium are
available to order as framed or mounted prints.

For details, contact:
THE FRANCIS FRITH COLLECTION

UK address: The Old Rectory, Bimport, Shaftesbury,
Dorset SP7 8AT
Tel: 01747 855 669   Fax: 01747 855 065
E-mail: sales@francisfrith.com

USA address: Frith USA Inc, 15740 Rockford Road,
#106 Plymouth MN 55446
Tel: 612 519 8446   Fax: 612 519 8662
E-mail: sales@francisfrith.com

47265 Cheltenham, High Street 1901

Contents

The photographs used in this book are organised alphabetically by town within the county boundaries which followed the 1974 local government reorganisation. For this reason some towns may be found in counties such as Avon, that were traditionally within Somerset. Other examples include towns listed under Humberside that once formed part of Yorkshire; and Middlesex towns that will be found in Greater London. Since the number of photographs for Scotland and Ireland are limited these are listed alphabetically by town.

As with any historical database the Frith Archive is constantly being corrected and improved and the publishers would welcome information on omissions or inaccuracies.

The Frith archive is acknowledged as being the only nationally important collection of period photographs of Britain still in private ownership. Its founder, Francis Frith, one of the greatest of the Victorian pioneers in photography, made it his life's work to make high quality topographical images of Britain available to the greatest number of people. This book offers you an introduction to his studio's work, but such is its scale, that even the 2,000 or more views included constitute less than one percent of the archive's entire content.

This Compendium can do much to enrich your life and outlook, offering you a unique opportunity to enter another world. From within our modern global culture it is hard for us to imagine how life must have been a hundred years ago. Through Frith's photographs you will find you can peel back the layers of history, experiencing Britain as it was in your parents' and grandparents' times, journeying deep into the Victorian era.

The world our ancestors knew was very different from our own. Our great grandparents lived in a time when many of today's sprawling commercial centres were still humble villages of a few hundred people; when market towns really were outlets for local produce; when the working man travelled only as far as a horse and cart would carry him in a day. His world was centred on his community, his parish or town boundary the breadth of his horizon. Having few visual records of the world outside at his disposal, his sense of history and geography was grounded in the oral tradition, in stories, local gossip, and what information he could glean about the outside world from the columns of contemporary newspapers.

The invention of the photograph was to change this parochial perspective forever. Photography only became widespread in the latter part of Victoria's reign. It followed the spreading of the rail network, which gradually linked our great cities with scattered communities throughout Britain. At last the Victorian working man was able to travel, and so gain tantalising glimpses of other worlds and other ways of living. On festive and high days he and his family might take a train to the coast. Such outings would be occasions to remember. Victorian holidaymakers wanted view souvenirs of their days out, and Francis Frith offered them high quality sepia photographs. These were a huge success. People pasted his scenes of sea fronts, monuments and beauty spots in albums to enjoy through the dark nights of winter. They must have seemed a revelation. Here at last were memories that did not have to be imagined. Here were memories they could actually see and share with their friends and family.

We tend to think of Frith's sepia views of historical Britain as nostalgic, for most of us use them to conjure up memories of favourite places in our own lives. They seem to depict a slower, softer world than our own, one where there was always time to stand and stare, and time to chat with acquaintances on the street corner.

Yet we must remember that they recorded the simple details of daily life in the Victorian era. Francis Frith was working in an age of explosive change, and certainly not viewing his world through nostalgic sepia spectacles. He was capturing the realities of the society that surrounded him. Fortunately for us, unlike many photographers of the period, Frith did not shirk from including in his images items that visually dated them such as people and vehicles, material that was generally felt to detract from artistic composition. Frith achieved fine images by incorporating these vital elements of everyday life. He has left us an extraordinary legacy, a wealth of visual data, chronicling changes in dress, transport, roads, buildings, housing, engineering and industry, landscape and social conditions, covering a period of well over a century.

Such social changes to tend go by unnoticed in our lives, for we are unable to stand back and gain a long perspective on them. It is ironic that the broad and revealing prospect of Victorian life that Frith offers us is one he himself probably never experienced. His 2,000 images of British life and heritage grant us a unique panoramic view of a vanished world that was, of course, the template for our own. Within it are contained myriad clues and pointers to the society we live in today.

The Victorian era was one of achievement, by engineers, scientists and businessmen, and Francis Frith's archive, which grew to be the biggest of its kind in the world, is one of its greatest. Despite his success in creating two very successful and profitable businesses, and his extraordinary expeditions to the Middle East, perhaps Frith's most significant achievement is as a recorder of everyday life and the changing topography of Britain. After his death in 1898 Frith & Co continued until 1970, the archive eventually comprising over a third of a million images of 7,000 cities, towns and villages.

This book will stimulate your memories of the various periods in your life. By browsing through its 2,000 historical photographic scenes of British cities, towns and villages you can rediscover the localities and places that have been important in your life. The opportunities for memories and associations are almost endless - the area where your family has its roots, where you were born, went to school and college, where you were married, and the many places where you have enjoyed family holidays and have lived and worked. Your family and friends, too, will gain great pleasure dipping into its pages, revisiting cities, towns and villages they recall with affection.

A103001, Almondsbury, c1955

B307013, Banwell, the Square c1955

73964, Bath, Union Street 1923

57749, Bathampton, Canal and George Inn 1907

B308019, Batheaston, High Street c1960

B309011, Bathford, Ashley Road c1955

B310009, Bishop Sutton, the Square c1955

B311006, Bitton, High Street c1960

B313001, Bleadon, the Village c1960

45654, Bristol, Park Street 1900

C230037, Chew Magna, Main Street c1965

50116, Chipping Sodbury, Horse Street 1903

C231022, Churchill, Clock Tower c1955

65406, Clevedon, Hill Road 1913

45555, Clifton, Bridge 1900

C143014, COMBE DOWN, THE AVENUE C1955

C233002, COMPTON MARTIN, POST OFFICE C1955

D88019, DUNDRY, MAIN STREET C1965

65415, EAST CLEVEDON, 1913

E65004, EAST HARPTREE, THE VILLAGE C1965

F70004, FARLEIGH, THE GEORGE INN C1955

F71008, FARRINGTON GURNEY, VILLAGE C1955

F72025, FELTON, THE CHURCH C1965

F74017, FRAMPTON COTTERELL, THE VILLAGE C1955

F48017, FRESHFORD, VILLAGE C1955

H165022, HINTON CHARTERHOUSE, C1955

H166002, HUTTON, THE VILLAGE C1965

K64003, KEYNSHAM, HIGH STREET 1950

M125005, MIDSOMER NORTON, HIGH STREET 1952

N65036, NAILSEA, HIGH STREET C1965

O42013, Olveston, the Church c1965

P140011, Pensford, the Village c1965

76002, Portishead, the Esplanade 1924

66584, Radstock, Valley and Railway 1914

S264045, Severn Bridge, Aust Ferry c1965

S270001, Shirehampton, High Street c1955

T107024, Thornbury, High Street 1954

W180024, Wellow, the Village c1965

W181019, West Harptree, the Village c1965

20323, Weston-super-Mare, 1887

7007, Widcombe, the Church c1874

38460, Worle, Village 1896

W186020, Wrington, Broad Street c1965

50124, Yate, Church and Schools 1903

Y47015, Yatton, High Street c1955

A158030, AMPTHILL, MARKET PLACE c1955

A161014, ASPLEY GUISE, THE SQUARE c1955

70423, BEDFORD, HIGH STREET 1921

77217, BIGGLESWADE, HITCHIN STREET 1925

39737, DUNSTABLE, HIGH STREET 1897

70452, ELSTOW, THE SWAN INN 1921

G141007, GREAT BARFORD, HIGH STREET c1955

L211032, LEIGHTON BUZZARD, MARKET DAY c1955

39700, LUTON, CORN EXCHANGE 1897

P130010, POTTON, THE SQUARE 1951

77225, SANDY, BEDFORD ROAD 1925

S378007, SHEFFORD, NORTH BRIDGE STREET 1951

S380002, STEPPINGLEY, THE VILLAGE c1955

39970, TURVEY, VILLAGE 1897

W300001, WOBURN, HIGH STREET c1955

50690, Ascot, 1903

B97001, Binfield, The Stag 1892

46895, Bracknell, High Street 1901

63821, Bray, Village 1911

59962, Caversham, Bridge Street 1908

77584, Cookham, High Street 1925

57016, Crowthorne, Village 1906

D9056, Datchet, High Street c1945

67007, Eton, College Barnes Pool 1914

57013, Finchampstead, Post Office 1906

61983, Holyport, Main Road 1909

49384, Hungerford, High Street 1903

63797, Maidenhead, High Street 1911

N61024, Newbury, Market Place 1952

62219, Pangbourne, Village 1910

74436, READING, BROAD STREET 1923

56999, SANDHURST, VILLAGE 1906

S256010, SLOUGH, CROWN CORNER C1955

52040, SONNING, VILLAGE 1904

52933, STREATLEY, VILLAGE 1904

S230024, SUNNINGHILL, STATION PARADE C1955

T254011, THEALE, HIGH STREET C1955

T48027, TILEHURST, SCHOOL ROAD C1960

W377001, WALTHAM ST LAWRENCE, THE VILLAGE C1955

42641, WARFIELD, THE VILLAGE 1899

27177, WARGRAVE, VILLAGE 1890

W549028, WEST ILSLEY, HIGH STREET C1955

66981, WINDSOR, CASTLE HILL 1914

57026, WOKINGHAM, BROAD STREET 1906

27246, WRAYSBURY, THE FERRY 1890

A148012, Amersham, High Street c1955

47462, Aylesbury, Market Square 1901

B439056, Bletchley, Bletchley Road c1960

43963, Bourne End, 1899

B280027, Buckingham, Market Place c1955

B250050, Burnham, High Street c1955

C498015, Chalfont St Giles, the Village c1955

C524007, Chalfont St Peter, High Street c1960

C609013, Chenies, the Village c1955

70536, Chesham, Market Square 1921

D183020, Denham, the Village c1965

F196022, Farnham Common, High Street c1965

F195008, Farnham Royal, the Village c1955

G228014, Gerrards Cross, the Highway 1957

G241026, Great Missenden, High Street 1952

27217, HAMBLEDON, THE LOCK 1890

70607, HIGH WYCOMBE, FROGMORE SQUARE 1921

L201025, LAVENDON, SQUARE C1965

L505311, LITTLE CHALFONT, C1955

L471014, LONG CRENDON, HIGH STREET 1962

23690, MARLOW, FISHERMAN'S RETREAT 1890

N62022, NEWPORT PAGNELL, HIGH STREET C1955

O118006, OVING, THE VILLAGE C1955

S685022, STOKENCHURCH, KINGS ARMS C1955

54109, TAPLOW, THE VILLAGE 1906

47469, WADDESDON, 1901

44771, WENDOVER, TRING ROAD 1899

W433013, WHITCHURCH, HIGH STREET C1955

W432030, WINSLOW, MARKET SQUARE C1960

62231, WOOBURN GREEN, THE VILLAGE 1910

B725013, BALSHAM, CAMBRIDGE ROAD c1955

B726009, BLUNTISHAM, HIGH STREET c1955

B713006, BOURN, HIGH STREET c1955

58560, BRAMPTON, VILLAGE 1907

55429, BUCKDEN, CHURCH STREET 1906

B728031, BURWELL, HIGH STREET c1955

84533, CAMBRIDGE, ST ANDREW'S STREET 1931

C584003, CASTOR, c1955

C210004, CHATTERIS, HIGH STREET c1955

E201303, EARITH, HIGH STREET c1955

55436, ELLINGTON, VILLAGE 1906

73583, ELM, VILLAGE 1923

78274, ELY, FORE HILL 1925

39994, EYNESBURY, ST MARY STREET 1897

F191016, FENSTANTON, THE GREEN c1955

F104002, Fulbourne, High Street c1950

G277007, Galmingay, Mill Street c1965

41270, Godmanchester, High Street 1898

81770, Grantchester, the Village 1929

G278009, Great Shelford, High Street c1955

G279009, Great Staughton, the Village c1955

H249003, Haddenham, High Street c1950

58555, Hartford, River and Anchor Inn 1907

44253, Hemingford Abbots, from the River 1899

66965, Hemingford Grey, Village 1914

H440023, Hilton, the Village Hall c1955

H441018, Hinxton, High Street c1960

H442003, Histon, High Street c1965

66968, Holywell, Village 1914

H443002, Horningsea, the Village c1955

66963, Houghton, Village 1914

81878, Huntingdon, High Street & George Hotel 1929

K157054, Kimbolton, High Street c1965

L459025, Linton, High Street c1955

L366010, Littleport, Main Street c1955

61523, Madingley, Village 1909

81911, March, 1929

M301010, Melbourn, High Street c1965

M302015, Meldreth, High Street c1965

55441, Offord Darcy, Village 1906

69094, Peterborough, Narrow Street 1919

R359059, Ramsey, High Street c1965

S671003, Sawston, High Street c1965

S597004, Soham, Stillyards c1955

55434, Somersham, Village 1906

55433, SPALDWICK, VILLAGE 1906

48068, ST IVES, MARKET PLACE 1901

39975, ST NEOTS, HIGH STREET 1897

S673010, STILTON, HIGH STREET C1955

S674004, SUTTON, HIGH STREET C1955

S678009, SWAFFHAM BULBECK, HIGH STREET C1955

S675017, SWAVESEY, HIGH STREET C1965

T298004, TEVERSHAM, HIGH STREET C1965

66910, TRUMPINGTON, VILLAGE 1914

73591, UPWELL, VILLAGE 1923

W508012, WARBOYS, HIGH STREET C1955

W509011, WATERBEACH, HIGH STREET C1955

W90014, WHITTLESEY, MARKET PLACE C1965

W510302, WILLINGHAM, HIGH STREET C1960

47580, WISBECH, MARKET PLACE 1901

5518P, ALDERNEY, VICTORIA STRÉET c1915

31558, GUERNSEY, ST PETER PORT OLD HARBOUR 1892

31561, GUERNSEY, ST PETER PORT CASTLE CORNET 1892

31562, GUERNSEY, ST PETER PORT ESPLANADE 1892

31596, GUERNSEY, ROCQUAINS CASTLE AND BAY 1893

44063, GUERNSEY, HARBOUR 1899

44086, GUERNSEY, COBO 1899

31628, JERSEY, ST HELIER HARBOUR 1893

31629, JERSEY, ST HELIER HARBOUR 1893

31632, JERSEY, ST AUBIN FROM THE PIER 1893

31634, JERSEY, ST AUBIN ESPLANADE 1893

31650, JERSEY, ST HELIER ROYAL YACHT HOTEL 1893

44091, JERSEY, GOREY AND MOUNT ORQUEIL 1899

33872, SARK, CREUX HARBOUR 1894

33873, SARK, BEL AIR HOTEL 1894

37447, ALDERLEY EDGE, LONDON ROAD 1896

A214021, ALSAGER, CREWE ROAD c1965

48663, ASTBURY, VILLAGE AND CHURCH 1902

B781008, BARTON UPON IRWELL, SHIP CANAL c1955

B519011, BOLLINGTON, PALMERSTON STREET c1955

40479, BOLLINGTON CROSS, VILLAGE 1897

49887, CHESTER, EASTGATE 1903

42154, CONGLETON, LAWTON STREET 1898

C316012, CREWE, MARKET STREET c1960

1722, ECCLESTON, FERRY c1886

F176059, FRODSHAM, HIGH STREET c1965

G200004, GRAPPENHALL, THE VILLAGE c1955

45439, HALTON, CASTLE 1900

42119, KNUTSFORD, ROSE AND CROWN 1898

40483, LYMM, THE CROSS 1897

42599, MACCLESFIELD, MARKET PLACE 1898

M237003, MIDDLEWICH, WHITE BEAR HOTEL c1955

42181, NANTWICH, WELSH ROW 1898

N88006, NESTON, HIGH STREET 1939

45422, NORTHWICH, SWING BRIDGE 1900

P255301, PARKGATE, c1955

37439, PRESTBURY, HIGH STREET 1896

82384, RUNCORN, THE TWO BRIDGES 1929

S489005, SANDBACH, WAR MEMORIAL c1955

39616, STYAL, QUARRY BANK MILL 1897

W29060, WARRINGTON, BRIDGE STREET c1955

W368001, WEAVERHAM, HIGH STREET c1955

59503, WIDNES, ST PAUL'S CHURCH & LIBRARY 1908

39604, WILMSLOW, GROVE STREET 1897

W561004, WINSFORD, WARTON HILL c1955

E170001, Easington, Village c1955

58660, Guisborough, Market Place 1907

30767, Hartlepool, Lighthouse 1892

L507005, Levenbridge, the Village c1955

54840, Marske-by-the-Sea, 1906

47980, Middlesbrough, Corporation Road 1901

O45001, Ormesby, High Street c1955

54874, Redcar, Queen Street 1906

74267, Saltburn-by-the-Sea, Promenade 1923

30786, Seaton Carew, Church Street 1892

S285028, Skelton, Village c1955

44740, Stockton-on-Tees, High Street 1899

T122001, Thornaby-on-Tees, Five Lamps 1957

46944, West Hartlepool, Church Street 1901

Y17019, Yarm, High Street c1960

24482, BODMIN, FORE STREET 1890

82882, BUDE, BELLE VUE 1929

84283, CADGWITH, BEACH 1931

51824, CALLINGTON, FORE STREET 1904

59702, CALSTOCK, VIADUCT 1908

56158, CAMELFORD, FORE STREET 1906

53050, CHARLESTOWN, HARBOUR 1904

87513, COVERACK, HARBOUR 1936

86710, CRANTOCK, VILLAGE 1935

61059, FALMOUTH, THE QUAY 1908

87531, FEOCK, THE VILLAGE 1936

21250, FOWEY, TOWN QUAY 1888

59709, GUNNISLAKE, 1908

83197, HELFORD PASSAGE, 1930

65939, HELSTON, COINAGE HALL STREET 1913

24269, KYNANCE COVE, 1890

31809A, LANDS END, LONGSHIPS LIGHTHOUSE 1893

87118, LAUNCESTON, THE SQUARE 1935

29876, LELANT, CHURCH LANE 1892

56300, LISKEARD, FORE STREET 1906

56398, LOOE, FORE STREET 1906

56419, LOSTWITHIEL, FORE STREET 1906

27558, MEVAGISSEY, FORE STREET 1890

79945, MOUSEHOLE, 1927

76638, MULLION, 1924

69744, NEWLYN, 1920

33522, NEWQUAY, HARBOUR 1894

56268, PADSTOW, MARKET PLACE 1906

69736, PENZANCE, MARKET JEW STREET 1920

47792, POLPERRO, HARBOUR 1901

78827, Port Isaac, The Village 1925

86570, Porthleven, Harbour 1935

41621, Redruth, Fore Street 1898

76023, Saltash, The Ferry 1924

2071, Scilly Isles, St Mary's c1864

28453, Scilly Isles, St Mary's Harbour 1891

31128A, Scilly Isles, St Mary's 1892

84124, St Austell, Fore Street 1931

56242, St Columb, Fair Street 1906

72849, St Ives, High Street 1922

88816, St Mawes, 1938

36179, St Michael's Mount, 1895

56178, Tintagel, The Village 1906

78415, Torpoint, Ferry 1925

64732, Truro, Boscawen Street 1912

A288028, ALLITHWAITE, THE VILLAGE c1950

A290055, ALSTON, MARKET CROSS c1955

64303, AMBLESIDE, WHITE LION HOTEL 1912

A291010, APPLEBY, c1955

28645, ARNSIDE, 1891

35913, BARDSEA, THE BEACH 1895

64405, BARROW-IN-FURNESS, DALTON ROAD 1912

38800, BOWNESS, FERRY BOAT 1896

B604301, BROUGH, MAIN STREET c1965

40515, CARK, HOUSE AND BRIDGE 1897

C211001, CARLISLE, MARKET PLACE c1935

67406, CARTMEL, CAVENDISH STREET 1914

C568001, CLEATOR MOOR, THE SQUARE c1960

54993, COCKERMOUTH, STATION STREET 1906

64281, CONISTON, WATERHEAD 1912

Cumbria

22139, CRUMMOCK WATER, FROM LOWESWATER 1889

75625, DENT, 1924

54982, DERWENT WATER, FRIARS CRAG & CAUSEY PIKE 1906

E192008, EGREMONT, MARKET PLACE c1960

40521, FLOOKBURGH, VILLAGE 1897

F183010, FRIZINGTON, MAIN STREET c1950

G259027, GARRIGILL, THE VILLAGE c1955

70656, GRANGE-OVER-SANDS, PROMENADE 1921

79206, GRASMERE, RED LION SQUARE 1926

H419007, HAVERTHWAITE, c1960

82372, HAWKSHEAD, MARKET SQUARE 1929

75795, KENDAL, THE MARKET 1924

K12073, KESWICK, DERWENT WATER c1955

67344, KIRKBY LONSDALE, 1914

K148015, KIRKBY STEPHEN, MARKET STREET c1960

K131032, KIRKOSWALD, THE VILLAGE c1965

L203005, LONGTOWN, HIGH STREET c1955

M317015, MARYPORT, SENHOUSE STREET c1955

M277001, MILLOM, MARKET SQUARE c1955

M263018, MILNTHORPE, THE SQUARE c1950

67414, NEWBY BRIDGE, 1914

32923, PENRITH, MARKET PLACE 1893

S652003, SCOTBY, MARKET HILL c1955

34077, SEDBERGH, MARKET PLACE 1894

64395, ULVERSTON, MARKET PLACE 1912

W497053, WETHERAL, THE VILLAGE c1955

W313030, WHITEHAVEN, MARKET PLACE c1965

W424033, WIGTON, THE SQUARE c1965

64319, WINDERMERE, ABOVE WATERHEAD 1912

W316014, WORKINGTON, OXFORD STREET c1955

A199017, ALFRETON, HIGH STREET c1955

A203022, AMBERGATE, THE VILLAGE c1955

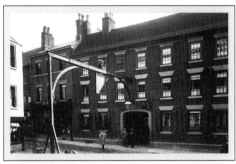

18577, ASHBOURNE, GREEN MAN 1886

67616, BAKEWELL, RUTLAND SQUARE 1914

B803025, BARLBOROUGH, HIGH STREET c1955

16576, BASLOW, BRIDGE c1883

B437020, BELPER, KING STREET 1951

B133038, BOLSOVER, MARKET PLACE c1955

B485013, BONSALL, THE CROSS c1955

B486011, BRADWELL, THE VILLAGE c1955

B603016, BRIMINGTON, HIGH STREET c1965

74118, BUXTON, SPRING GARDENS 1923

61777, CASTLETON, MARKET PLACE 1909

18644, CHATSWORTH HOUSE, 1886

48884, CHESTERFIELD, HIGH STREET 1902

C403009, CLOWNE, MILL STREET c1950

37778, DERBY, VICTORIA STREET 1896

D159020, DUFFIELD, TOWN STREET c1955

E226002, ECKINGTON, HIGH STREET c1955

37812, EYAM, VILLAGE 1896

F127003, FINDERN, THE GREEN c1965

G182028, GRINDLEFORD, c1960

H330106, HARTINGTON, VILLAGE c1955

48914, HATHERSAGE, VILLAGE 1902

H331014, HEANOR, THE CHURCH c1960

85261, HOPE, THE SMITHY 1932

I37042, ILKESTON, BATH STREET c1949

L198002, LONG EATON, HIGH STREET 1950

M343027, MAPPLETON, THE VILLAGE c1955

31274, MATLOCK BATH, 1892

M220001, MICKLEOVER, THE VILLAGE c1955

37820, MIDDLETON DALE, ENTRANCE & LOVERS LEAP 1896

67598, MILLER'S DALE, VILLAGE 1914

N126030, NEW MILLS, MARKET STREET c1965

O129008, OLD WHITTINGTON, HIGH STREET c1955

R298026, REPTON, HIGH STREET c1955

18617, ROWSLEY, PEACOCK INN 1886

S725004, SOUTH NORMANTON, MARKET PLACE c1955

S454008, SWADLINCOTE, HIGH STREET c1955

T46001, TIDESWELL, QUEEN STREET c1960

T204029, TINTWISTLE, OLD ROAD c1960

31300, VIA GELLIA, 'PIG OF LEAD' INN 1892

41135, WHALEY BRIDGE, THE SCHOOL 1898

W349003, WHITWELL, HIGH STREET 1952

W557001, WILLINGTON, THE VILLAGE c1955

55971, Abbotsham, Village 1906

75145, Appledore, Quay 1923

73181, Ashburton, East Street and Bull Ring 1922

48454, Axminster, South Street 1902

68547, Babbacombe, Downs 1918

33422, Barnstaple, High Street 1894

72943, Beer, 1922

42263, Bere Alston, 1898

69331, Bideford, the Promenade 1919

78342, Bigbury-on-Sea, the Village 1925

24886, Bishops Tawton, 1890

58522, Bovey Tracey, Coach for the Moors 1907

42438, Branscombe, the Village 1898

45686, Braunton, North Street 1900

63861, Brendon, the Village 1911

78490, BRIXHAM, HARBOUR 1925

68726, BUDLEIGH SALTERTON, HIGH STREET 1918

73124, CHAGFORD, THE SQUARE 1922

24769, CLOVELLY, 1890

78534, COMBE CELLARS, 1925

63962, COMBE MARTIN, 1911

53981, COUNTESS WEAR, BRIDGE 1906

59406, COUNTISBURY, THE BLUE BALL INN 1907

37634, CREDITON, HIGH STREET 1896

21650, DARTMOUTH, REGATTA 1889

72990, DAWLISH, THE BEACH 1922

22446, DEVONPORT, ROYAL HOTEL 1890

78374, DITTISHAM, RIVER DART FROM MANOR STREET 1925

88621, EAST BUDLEIGH, VILLAGE 1938

38010, EXETER, HIGH STREET 1896

36055, Exmouth, Rolle Street 1895

52461, Frogmore, Village 1904

33425, Goodleigh, Village 1894

31321, Hawkchurch, Church and Village 1892

H161006, Holsworthy, the Square c1955

H111024, Honiton, High Street c1955

52467, Hope Cove, 1904

I50001, Ilfracombe, the Harbour c1890

69337, Instow, Foreshore 1919

22522, Ivybridge, Old Church 1890

53986, Kenton, the Village 1906

38429, Kingsbridge, Fore Street 1896

56067, Lydford, the Village 1906

43095, Lynmouth, Pier 1899

79903, Malborough, Lower Town 1927

56604, Moretonhampstead, Church Street 1906

56572, Newton Abbot, St Leonard's Tower 1906

83975, Newton Ferrers, Bridge End 1931

24835, Northam, Village 1890

22590, Okehampton, Fore Street Market 1890

56671, Otterton, Village 1906

58182, Ottery St Mary, Market Place 1907

74719, Paignton, Church Street 1923

22474, Plymouth, Barbican 1890

41943, Plympton, St Mary Fore Street 1898

38483, Salcombe, Quayside 1896

36081, Seaton, Fore Street 1895

73108A, Shaldon, Fore Street 1922

53807, Sidmouth, High Street 1906

78256, Strete, the Village 1925

45724, Swimbridge, 1900

75113, Taddiport, the Village 1923

22546, Tavistock, Duke Street 1890

49559, Teignmouth, Parade 1903

68605, Thurlestone, Village 1918

69888, Tiverton, Castle Street 1920

53993, Topsham, the Strand 1906

54027, Torquay, Fleet Street 1906

32334, Torrington, Market Place 1893

38228, Totnes, High Street 1896

62287, Walkhampton, the Village 1910

24854, Weare Giffard, Bridge 1890

53995, Woodbury, 1906

25269, Woodleigh, Church Porch and Cottages 1890

43130, Woolacombe, 1899

A Victorian Pioneer

The photograph opposite offers some clues to the complex and multitudinous character of Francis Frith, founder of the world famous photographic archive. Here we see him in flamboyant mode, garbed in Arab dress. Yet Frith was also a devout Quaker and a highly successful and respected Victorian businessman, and this more orthodox and sober side of his personality is reflected in the stiff, formal photograph in the introduction to this book.

By 1855 Frith had already established a wholesale grocery business in Liverpool and sold it for an astonishing £200,000, the equivalent of over £15,000,000 today. Now a multi-millionaire, Francis Frith was able to indulge his irresistible desire to travel. As a child he had pored over books penned by early explorers, and his imagination had been stirred by family holidays to the sublime mountain regions of Wales and Scotland. 'What a land of spirit-stirring and enriching scenes and places!' he had written. He was to return to these scenes of grandeur in later years to 'recapture the thousand vivid and tender memories', but with a very different purpose. Now in his thirties, and captivated by the new science of photography, Frith set out on a series of pioneering journeys to the Middle East, that occupied him from 1856 until 1860.

He took with him a specially-designed wicker carriage which acted as camera, dark-room and sleeping chamber. These far-flung journeys were filled with intrigue and adventure. In his life story, written when he was sixty-three, Frith tells of being held captive by bandits, and fighting 'an awful midnight battle to the very point of exhaustion and surrender with a deadly pack of hungry, wild dogs'. He bargained for several weeks with a 'mysterious priest' over a beautiful seven-volume illuminated Koran, which is now in the British Museum. Wearing full Arab costume, Frith arrived at Akaba by camel seventy years before Lawrence of Arabia, where he encountered 'desert princes and rival sheikhs, blazing with jewel-hilted swords'.

During these extraordinary adventures he was assiduously exploring the desert regions of the Nile and recording the antiquities and people with his camera. Frith was the first photographer ever to travel beyond the sixth cataract. Africa, we must remember, was still the 'Dark Continent', and Stanley and Livingstone's famous meeting was a decade into the future. The conditions for picture-taking confound belief. He laboured for hours on end in his dark-room in the sweltering heat, while the volatile collodion chemicals fizzed dangerously in their trays. Often he was forced to work in tombs and caves where conditions were cooler.

Back in London he exhibited his photographs and was 'rapturously cheered' by the Royal Society. His reputation as a photographer was made overnight. His photographs were issued in albums by James S Virtue and William MacKenzie, and published simultaneously in London and New York. An eminent historian has likened their impact on the population at the time to that on our own generation of the first photographs taken on the surface of the moon.

Characteristically, Frith spotted the potential to create a new business as a specialist publisher of photographs. In 1860 he married Mary Ann Rosling and set out to photograph every city, town and village in Britain. For the next thirty years Frith travelled the country by train and by pony and trap, producing photographs that were keenly bought by the millions of Victorians who, because of the burgeoning rail network, were beginning to enjoy holidays and day trips to Britain's seaside resorts and beauty spots.

To meet the demand he gathered together a team of up to twelve photographers, and also published the work of independent artist-photographers of the reputation of Roger Fenton and Francis Bedford. Together with clerks and photographic printers he employed a substantial staff at his Reigate studios. To gain an understanding of the scale of Frith's business one only has to look at the catalogue issued by Frith & Co in 1886. It runs to some 670 pages, listing not only many thousands of views of the British Isles but also photographs of most major European countries, and China, Japan, the USA and Canada. By 1890 Frith had created the greatest specialist photographic publishing company in the world.

He died in 1898 at his villa in Cannes, his great project still growing. His sons, Eustace and Cyril, took over the task, and Frith & Co continued in business for another seventy years, until by 1970 the archive contained over a third of a million pictures of 7,000 cities, towns and villages.

The photographic record he has left to us stands as a living monument to a remarkable and very special man.

The dhow in which Francis Frith travelled, moored on the Nile at Ibrim

A2025, Abbotsbury, Market Street c1955

48399, Allington, Village 1902

58134, Beaminster, Market Place 1907

B480019, Bere Regis, The Village c1955

B282001, Blandford Forum, 1900

31380, Boscombe, The Arcade 1892

52767, Bothenhampton, 1904

52874, Bournemouth, The Square 1904

40093, Bradpole, The Village 1897

52756, Bridport, East Street 1904

48412, Burton Bradstock, The Village 1902

52484, Canford, Village 1904

72757, Charminster, The Village 1922

27380, Charmouth, 1890

65080, Chideock, Village 1912

C222001, CHILD OKEFORD, 1900

45053, CHRISTCHURCH, CHURCH STREET 1900

C160015, CORFE CASTLE, THE VILLAGE & CASTLE c1955

C694011, CRANBORNE, THE VILLAGE c1955

83390, DORCHESTER, HIGH WEST STREET 1930

52722, EAST LULWORTH, THE VILLAGE 1904

E128015, EVERSHOT, FORE STREET c1965

F125008, FONTMELL MAGNA, c1955

54584, FRAMPTON, VILLAGE 1906

54575, FROME VAUCHURCH, 1906

H295017, HIGHCLIFFE, LYMINGTON ROAD c1955

L469032, LANGTON MATRAVERS, HIGH STREET c1965

50496, LODERS, THE VILLAGE 1903

78804, LULWORTH, THE STEAMSHIP 1925

45242, LYME REGIS, BROAD STREET 1900

54563, Maiden Newton, Dorchester Road 1906

M185032, Marnhull, Post Office and Village c1955

M216019, Melbury Osmond, the Village c1955

M217003, Melcombe Bingham, Hartfoot Lane c1955

65063, Melplash, the Village 1912

M80049, Milton Abbas, the Village c1955

52774, Morcombelake, the Village 1904

M308008, Moreton, the Post Office c1955

M106035, Mudeford, Harbour c1955

48440, Netherbury, Village 1902

O117031, Okeford Fitzpaine, High Street c1955

61171, Poole, Barges and Quay 1908

34551, Portland, 1894

54548, Puncknowle, Village 1906

S593052, Shaftesbury, Gold Hill c1955

51329, Sherborne, Half Moon Street 1904

S447002, Stoborough, Village c1955

78796, Studland, Beach 1925

78794, Swanage, Station Road 1925

62580, Sydling St Nicholas, Village 1910

83360, Symondsbury, Village 1930

54556, Toller Porcorum, Village 1906

U13011, Upwey, c1950

W173034, Wareham, North Street 1949

40081, West Bay, the Quay 1897

68071, Westbourne, 1918

73952, Weymouth, from the north 1923

62270, Whitchurch Canonicorum, Village 1910

52472, Wimborne, High Street 1904

52739, Witchampton, Village 1904

A111001, Annfield Plain, Front Street 1951

67169, Barnard Castle, 1914

74338, Bishop Auckland, Newgate Street 1923

B327050, Blackhall, Middle Street c1965

67122, Brancepeth, Castle 1914

18830, Castle Eden, Dene 1886

C246001, Chester-le-Street, the Market Place c1955

41446, Cotherstone, Village 1898

C249005, Coxhoe, Blackgate c1955

C250019, Crook, Hope Street c1955

D91010, Daddry Shield, the Village c1955

54444, Darlington, Bond Gate 1906

67127, Durham, Old Elvet 1914

E71027, Easington Colliery, c1955

F81022, Ferryhill, Darlington Road 1959

30724, Finchale Priory, 1892

F82002, Frosterley, Front Street c1955

30715, Lambton Castle, 1892

L162010, Langley Moor, Village 1951

32330, Raby Castle, from the south east 1893

41447, Romaldkirk, Village 1898

S287070, Seaham, Church Street c1965

S288015, Sedgefield, High Street c1968

S704006, Shildon, Church Street c1965

S295007, St John's Chapel, Market Place c1955

S292001, Staindrop, the Village c1955

S293054, Stanhope, Front Street c1965

W247024, Willington, High Street 1962

W536023, Wingate, Main Street c1965

W210016, Wolsingham, Market Place c1955

A106015, ABRIDGE, MARKET PLACE c1965

A107006, ALTHORNE, THE CORNER c1965

B438003, BASILDON, MARKET PLACE 1961

B319079, BILLERICAY, HIGH STREET c1955

62127, BLACK NOTLEY, 1909

B320009, BLACKMORE, THE VILLAGE c1955

48279, BOCKING, BRAYFORD STREET 1902

55533, BRAINTREE, HIGH STREET 1906

50222, BRENTWOOD, HIGH STREET 1903

B209022, BRIGHTLINGSEA, HIGH STREET c1955

B324007, BURES, c1960

C238001, CASTLE HEDINGHAM, THE VILLAGE c1955

41504, CHELMSFORD, HIGH STREET 1898

78722, CHIGWELL, THE VILLAGE 1925

51537, CLACTON-ON-SEA, STATION ROAD 1904

C242056, Coggeshall, Tilkey Road c1965

48299, Colchester, High Street 1902

C243023, Corringham, Church Road c1955

62124, Cressing, 1909

50235, Danbury, 1903

D51004, Dovercourt, High Street c1955

60600, East Horndon, Blacksmith Row 1908

70132, Epping, High Street 1921

50569, Finchingfield, 1903

57561, Fingringhoe, 1907

70307, Frinton-on-Sea, Connaught Avenue 1921

G85042, Grays, High Street c1965

48290, Great Bentley, Village 1902

G95001, Great Easton, the Ford 1951

G100002, Great Wakering, High Street c1955

H168011, HALSTEAD, HIGH STREET c1955

51086, HARLOW, VILLAGE 1903

H150009, HARWICH, CHURCH STREET 1954

H173016, HATFIELD PEVEREL, POST OFFICE c1965

78741, INGATESTONE, HIGH STREET 1925

60599, INGRAVE, VILLAGE 1908

78736, KELVEDON, HIGH STREET 1925

29066, LEIGH-ON-SEA, 1891

52361, LEXDEN, VILLAGE 1904

73923, LOUGHTON, WAR MEMORIAL 1923

46711, MALDON, HIGH STREET 1901

85126, NEWPORT, VILLAGE 1932

74823, ONGAR, HIGH STREET 1923

29074, PRITTLEWELL, VILLAGE 1891

R224027, RAYLEIGH, TOWN CENTRE 1957

46725, Rayne, Village 1901

R226028, Rochford, North Street c1965

65087, Saffron Walden, 1912

S280006, South Ockendon, South Road c1955

54466, South Weald, Church and Village 1906

41377, Southend, Pier 1898

64263, St Osyth, Village 1912

S258033, Stanford le Hope, King Street c1960

55458, Thaxted, Old Guildhall 1906

70160, Waltham Abbey, 1921

70290, Walton on the Naze, High Street 1921

W189006, West Horndon, Thorndon Avenue c1965

W195069, Wickford, High Street c1965

46223, Witham, High Street 1900

57557, Wyvenhoe, 1907

47357, Amberley, 1901

51750, Berkeley, Market Place 1904

59062, Birdlip, George Hotel 1907

62697, Bisley, High Street 1910

B392035, Bourton-on-the-Water, 1948

62690, Brimscombe, 1910

B533032, Brockweir, the Village c1955

62713, Chalford, 1910

47265, Cheltenham, High Street 1901

C335035, Chipping Campden, High Street c1955

C448016, Cinderford, the Square c1955

40971, Cirencester, Castle Street 1898

C315019, Coleford, Town Centre 1950

D72031, Dursley, Long Street c1955

51987, Gloucester, Southgate Street 1904

H338017, HUNTLEY, HIGH STREET c1955

L200008, LYDNEY, NEWERNE STREET c1950

N1004, NAILSWORTH, BRIDGE STREET c1955

N87048, NEWNHAM, HIGH STREET c1955

N125013, NORTHLEACH, MARKET SQUARE c1955

R311007, RODBOROUGH, THE VILLAGE c1955

S502004, SHARPNESS, DOCKS AND SEVERN BRIDGE c1955

S265010, STONEHOUSE, HIGH STREET c1955

S260045, STOW-ON-THE-WOLD, THE SQUARE 1957

77562, STROUD, KING STREET 1925

T155027, TETBURY, CHURCH STREET c1949

59072, TEWKESBURY, CHURCH STREET 1907

51953, ULEY, GREEN AND CHURCH 1904

W378017, WINCHCOMBE, HIGH STREET c1960

39382, WOTTON-UNDER-EDGE, LONG STREET 1897

A4009, Abbotts Ann, the Village c1955

31112, Aldershot, Wellington Street 1892

A181009, Alresford, West Street c1955

79440, Alton, High Street 1927

42721, Alverstoke, the Crescent 1898

42092, Amport, Village 1898

60092, Andover, High Street 1908

52129, Basingstoke, Church Street 1904

82436, Bentley, 1929

B612014, Bishops Waltham, High Street 1957

57003, Blackwater, 1906

68814, Bordon, 1919

B544002, Botley, the Square c1955

B696013, Bramley, the Village c1960

46580, Bramshott, the Village 1901

B394006, BROCKENHURST, THE VILLAGE c1955

B43045, BUCKLERS HARD, THE VILLAGE c1960

41369, BURITON, CHURCH 1898

B647015, BURLEY, THE VILLAGE c1955

85061, CADNAM, TWIN OAKS 1932

C490017, CHANDLERS FORD, THE PARADE c1960

40739, CHAWTON, VILLAGE 1897

C573007, CHERITON, THE VILLAGE c1955

C227018, CHILBOLTON, VILLAGE c1965

53379, CHILWORTH, VILLAGE 1906

63035, CHURCH CROOKHAM, SANDY LANE 1910

C574001, CLANFIELD, THE VILLAGE c1955

62079, COVE, 1909

56344, CRONDALL, VILLAGE 1906

D181011, DENMEAD, HAMBLEDON ROAD c1960

E173016, EAST MEON, CHURCH STREET c1965

E167012, EASTLEIGH, LEIGH ROAD c1960

E62083, EMSWORTH, HIGH STREET c1965

57011, EVERSLEY, 1906

F103019, FAREHAM, WEST STREET c1960

68913, FARNBOROUGH, LYNCHFORD ROAD 1919

57430, FLEET, MARKET PLACE 1907

F178012, FORDINGBRIDGE, HIGH STREET c1960

F188003, FROXFIELD, STORES AND POST OFFICE c1960

86978, GRAYSHOTT, POST OFFICE 1935

49213, GREYWELL, VILLAGE 1903

H148121, HAMBLE, THE VILLAGE c1955

51894, HAMBLEDON, VILLAGE 1904

51235, HARTLEY WINTNEY, THE VILLAGE 1904

H147006, HAVANT, NORTH STREET c1955

57004, Hawley, Village 1906

46593, Headley, the Village 1901

42272, Holybourne, Village 1898

H403025, Horndean, the Square c1960

51450, Houghton, the Village 1904

H417005, Hurstbourne Tarrant, Village c1955

H372021, Hythe, High Street c1955

K99002, Kings Somborne, Village c1955

K140028, Kingsclere, Market Square c1955

75394, Liphook, Royal Anchor Hotel 1924

46610, Liss, 1901

L148045, Lymington, High Street 1952

60104, Lyndhurst, High Street 1908

N156001, Nether Wallop, the Square c1955

N58001, New Milton, 1910

51325, North Warnborough, the Village 1904

O111001, Oakley, Post Office Corner c1955

75277, Odiham, George Hotel 1924

P48007, Petersfield, Market Place c1950

30029, Portsea, Pier 1892

22751, Portsmouth, the Hard 1890

45027, Ringwood, Millstream 1900

51431, Romsey, Market Place 1904

41346, Sheet, Green 1898

60420, Southampton, High Street 1908

30018, Southsea, Sea Front 1892

S259081, Stockbridge, High Street 1957

43693, Upper Clatford, Village 1899

46353, Wherwell, Village 1901

80885, Winchester, High Street 1928

Francis Frith lived in an era of immense and sometimes violent change. For the poor in the early part of Victoria's reign work was a drudge and the hours interminable. The average working day began at five and, with no public holidays, people had precious little free time to enjoy themselves. Most had no transport other than a cart or gig at their disposal, and had not travelled far beyond the boundaries of their own town or village. However, by the 1870s, developments were well underway: the railways had threaded their way across the country, and Bank Holidays and half-day Saturdays had been made obligatory for all workers by Act of Parliament. It seemed that all of a sudden the working man and his family were able to enjoy days out and to see a little more of the world. We can only imagine the difference this made to their lives and outlook.

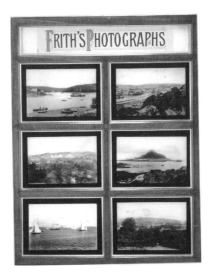

Francis Frith, with characteristic business acumen, foresaw that these new tourists would enjoy having souvenirs to commemorate their days out. He produced sepia photographic prints showing seaside resorts and other beauty spots. These were issued in three sizes, Royal (8½ x 6½ ins), Panoramic (11 x 7 ins) and Imperial (12 x 8 ins), on albumen photographic paper. Frith's pictures became very popular, and were keenly purchased by holidaymakers as view souvenirs. They were painstakingly pasted into family albums, which the Victorians pored over during the dark nights of winter to rekindle precious memories of their summer excursions. Many of these albums were beautifully decorated with flowers and motifs, as well as mementoes of happy occasions such as theatre tickets and fragments of favourite verse and doggerel. These early view mementoes can in one way be compared to our own albums of family 'snaps'. Yet the time of the family Box Brownie was still decades ahead, and photography was the exclusive province of the professional.

The photographic studio Francis Frith established at Reigate was soon supplying photographs to retail shops all over the country. In the late 1880s Frith & Co had become the greatest company of its kind in the world, with 2,000 shops selling his photographs - more outlets than the combined number that Boots and WH Smith have today. The archive still contains photographs of several of the stockists who sold Frith & Co views. On this page is a view of the Frith stockist at Ingelton in the Yorkshire Dales. Frith & Co's ornate mahogany display case, like this one, can be seen to the left of the window. These cases were beautifully made with mahogany frames and gilt inserts, and could display between six and eight pictures for sale. The other photograph on this page shows one of the Frith & Co display cases still in the archive's possession.

Later on during the Victorian era new high-quality mass-printing processes were patented that were to revolutionise the photographic industry. Francis Frith, ever at the forefront of technological change, began to have his souvenir views printed in Saxony, Germany, in numbers that ran into hundreds of thousands. These new inexpensive prints were the forerunners of today's postcards. So successful were these new cards that Frith established his own printing company, the Cotswold Collotype Company, in Gloucestershire.

The postcard took many years to develop into the form we would recognise today. In 1870 the Post Office issued the first plain cards, with a pre-printed stamp on one face. In 1894 they allowed other publishers' cards to be sent through the mail with an attached adhesive halfpenny stamp. Demand grew rapidly and the industry expanded. In 1895 a new size of postcard was permitted called the court card, measuring 4¾ x 3½ inches. There was little room for any illustration, for only one face could be used, and most of the available space was taken up by the sender's message. In 1899, the year after Frith's death, a new card measuring 5½ x 3½ inches became the standard format, but it was not until 1902 that the divided back came into being, with the address and message on one face and a full-size illustration on the other. The Victorian postal service was highly efficient, and a card sent today would invariably arrive early tomorrow. It is not surprising that postcards became a daily event in most people's lives, and the most effective means of communicating news and other urgent information.

Frith & Co, which had been in the vanguard of postcard development, became one of foremost publishers in the world, realising its founder's dream of making his photographs available to the greatest number of people.

26330 The Frith stockist at Ingelton in the Yorkshire Dales.

B417005, Barnt Green, The Village c1960

84620, Bewdley, Load Street 1931

B419011, Blakedown, Birmingham Road c1965

B423040, Bredon, The Village c1955

44111, Broadway, The Village 1899

84648, Bromsgrove, High Street 1931

B229039, Bromyard, High Street c1955

47321, Cropthorne, 1901

51938, Droitwich, High Street 1904

31106, Evesham, Bridge Street 1892

43989, Great Malvern, from Church Tower 1899

29288, Hereford, 1891

59104, Holt Fleet, 1907

62358, Kempsey, 1910

84610, Kidderminster, Town Hall 1931

K98030, KINGTON, THE CROSS C1955

51920, LEOMINSTER, HIGH STREET 1904

44016, OMBERSLEY, VILLAGE 1899

P172017, PEMBRIDGE, THE VILLAGE C1965

84678, PERSHORE, BRIDGE STREET 1931

R84057, REDDITCH, EVESHAM STREET 1967

54484, ROSS-ON-WYE, HIGH STREET 1906

R260003, RUBERY, THE SHOPPING CENTRE 1940

S214027, STOURPORT-ON-SEVERN, BRIDGE STREET C1955

32441, SYMONDS YAT, DOWARD HILL 1893

41722, TENBURY WELLS, TEME STREET 1898

A164001, UPPER ARLEY, FERRY AND VILLAGE C1955

84659, UPTON-ON-SEVERN, THE BRIDGE 1931

29321, WORCESTER, FRIAR STREET 1891

W312004, WYRE PIDDLE, C1955

A149007, Ashwell, High Street c1955

A99009, Ayot St Lawrence, the Village c1955

77099, Baldock, White Horse Street 1925

B407013, Berkhamsted, High Street c1955

61338, Bishops Stortford, North Street 1909

81852, Buntingford, High Street 1929

C320025, Codicote, the Village c1960

39730, Harpenden, Village 1897

H254008, Hatfield, St Albans Road c1955

H255046, Hemel Hempstead, the Marlowes c1965

71852, Hertford, Fore Street 1922

49736, Hitchin, High Street 1903

H259025, Hoddesdon, High Street c1955

49749, Ickleford, the Village 1903

K94007, Kimpton, High Street c1965

77105, LETCHWORTH, LEY'S AVENUE 1925

N153006, NEW MILL, THE VILLAGE C1955

N196015, NORTON, THE VILLAGE C1955

R87036, REDBOURN, HIGH STREET C1965

39675, RICKMANSWORTH, CHURCH STREET 1897

51095, SAWBRIDGEWORTH, KNIGHT STREET 1903

70477, ST ALBANS, CLOCK TOWER & MARKET CROSS 1921

81862, STANSTEAD ABBOTS, HIGH STREET 1929

44259, STEVENAGE, HIGH STREET AND GREEN 1899

T81001, TRING, HIGH STREET 1897

70172, WALTHAM CROSS, HIGH STREET 1921

77108, WARE, HIGH STREET 1925

70489, WATFORD, HIGH STREET 1921

W294055, WELWYN GARDEN CITY, STONE HILLS C1960

W296013, WHEATHAMPSTEAD, HIGH STREET C1961

A316013, Aldbrough, Hornsea Road c1955

B664002, Beeford, Crossroads c1960

86109, Beverley, Market Place 1934

39371, Bridlington, Princes Street 1897

B294011, Brigg, Wrawby Street 1954

B765016, Brough, Station Road c1960

B431014, Broughton, High Street c1965

55736, Cleethorpes, 1906

80139, Flamborough, Head North Landing 1927

52167, Frodingham, 1904

D179016, Great Driffield, Market Place c1960

26725, Grimsby, Corn Exchange & Market Place 1890

49807, Hull, Dock Offices 1903

49009, Scunthorpe, High Street 1902

44754, Spurn Head, Lighthouse 1899

36752, BALLAUGH, VILLAGE 1895

33024, CASTLETOWN, FROM THE PIER 1893

39899, COLBY, VILLAGE 1897

39882, DOUGLAS, PROMENADE 1897

33055, GLEN HELEN, 1893

36750, GLEN WILLYN, VILLAGE 1895

36755, GLENMAYE, 1895

59179, LAXEY, WHEEL 1907

36733, MAUGHOLD, VILLAGE 1895

33047, PEEL, CASTLE 1893

47239, PORT ERIN, FROM THE CLIFF 1901

33026, PORT SODERIC, BEACH 1893

39908, PORT ST MARY, 1895

36743, RAMSEY, PROMENADE 1895

39890, SNAEFELL, TRAIN AT SUMMIT 1897

B64020, BEMBRIDGE, HIGH STREET c1955

74688, BRADING, VILLAGE 1923

C439011, CALBOURNE, THE VILLAGE c1955

66311, COWES, 1913

74727, FRESHWATER, VILLAGE 1923

30066, NEWPORT, HIGH STREET 1892

53166, RYDE, UNION STREET 1904

36249, SANDOWN, ESPLANADE 1895

68264, SEAVIEW, HIGH STREET 1918

S496024, SHALFLEET, THE VILLAGE c1955

37239, SHANKLIN, THE VILLAGE 1896

S414007, SHORWELL, THE VILLAGE 1951

T65041, TOTLAND BAY, THE VILLAGE c1955

43133, VENTNOR, 1899

74740, YARMOUTH, 1923

53444, Ashford, High Street 1906

41549, Aylesford, 1898

46447, Benenden, Village 1901

46456, Biddenden, the Village 1901

61577, Bilsington, 1909

49416, Bishopsbourne, 1903

47631, Borough Green, 1901

B577002, Boxley, c1955

49399, Bridge, High Street 1903

48842, Broadstairs, Promenade 1902

70328, Canterbury, High Street 1921

47576, Charing, High Street 1901

60303, Chartham, Village 1908

50388, Cheriton, 1903

50340, Chilham, the Square 1903

77020, CRANBROOK, HIGH STREET 1925

49018, DARTFORD, SPITAL STREET 1902

44208, DEAL, ESPLANADE 1899

D50012, DOVER, CASTLE STREET C1955

D74011, DYMCHURCH, MARINE TERRACE C1955

E154006, EASTRY, HIGH STREET C1960

54271, EDENBRIDGE, HIGH STREET 1906

53250, EYNSFORD, 1905

E158025, EYTHORNE, SANDWICH ROAD C1955

31470, FAVERSHAM, WEST STREET 1892

64993, FOLKESTONE, BANDSTAND 1912

61565, GODMERSHAM, 1909

52537, GOUDHURST, VILLAGE 1904

49026, GRAVESEND, CLOCK TOWER 1902

60337, GREAT CHART, VILLAGE 1908

48255, HAWKHURST, MOOR HILL 1902

80116, HERNE BAY, THE BANDSTAND 1927

53553, HEVER, HENRY VIII 1906

H354013, HIGH HALDEN, THE VILLAGE C1955

H356015, HOO, THE VILLAGE C1955

50553, HORSMONDEN, THE GREEN 1903

44785, HYTHE, HIGH STREET 1899

47624, IGHTHAM, VILLAGE 1901

31500, LEEDS CASTLE, 1892

L322009, LENHAM, THE SQUARE C1955

49427, LITTLEBOURNE, VILLAGE 1903

L331002, LOWER STOKE, THE VILLAGE C1955

12684, MAIDSTONE, MARKET PLACE 1885

68432, MARGATE, QUEEN'S PROMENADE 1918

M253019, MEOPHAM, GREEN C1965

M86020, MINSTER, THE SQUARE C1955

N143001, NORTHFLEET, HIGH STREET C1955

58296, PEGWELL, VILLAGE 1907

P36034, PENSHURST, VILLAGE C1955

46408, PLAXTOL, VILLAGE 1901

Q4003, QUEENBOROUGH, HARBOURSIDE 1952

48028, RAMSGATE, HARBOUR 1901

59875, ROCHESTER, HIGH STREET 1908

48830, SALTWOOD, CASTLE 1902

56953, SANDGATE, HIGH STREET 1906

S60018, SANDWICH, THE BARBICAN C1955

44904, SEVENOAKS, HIGH STREET 1900

S528048, SHEERNESS, ESPLANADE AND BEACH C1955

48237, SISSINGHURST, 1902

S531004, SITTINGBOURNE, HIGH STREET C1955

S533021, Smarden, c1955

44805, St Margaret's Bay, 1899

51109, Stansted, Village 1903

51070, Staplehurst, 1903

44220, Sturry, Street and Post Office 1899

44994, Tenterden, High Street 1900

T101004, Tonbridge, High Street 1890

T87001, Tunbridge Wells, the Pantiles 1890

56929, Walmer, Promenade 1906

W61021, Westerham, Market Square c1955

27463, Westgate on Sea, Hotels and Beach 1890

W405026, Whitstable, Harbour Street 1959

61558, Willesborough, Windmill & Schools 1909

W155022, Wrotham, Village c1960

W157052, Wye, Church Street c1955

43496, ACCRINGTON, BLACKBURN ROAD 1899

74210, ANSDELL, FAIRHAVEN HOTEL 1923

B588050, BACCUP, ST JAMES STREET 1961

35726, BLACKBURN, SUDELL CROSS 1895

22893, BLACKPOOL, TALBOT SQUARE 1890

35789, BURNLEY, MANCHESTER ROAD 1895

54220, CARNFORTH, MARKET STREET 1906

71177, CHATBURN, THE VILLAGE 1921

71136, CLITHEROE, CASTLE ENTRANCE 1921

D8010, DARWEN, THE CIRCUS c1955

34357, DOWNHAM, THE VILLAGE 1894

41014, FLEETWOOD, WEST STREET 1898

G238007, GARSTANG, HIGH STREET c1955

71203, GISBURN, 1921

71152, GREAT MITTON, POST OFFICE & CHURCH 1921

71173, GRINDLETON, VILLAGE AND POST OFFICE 1921

46259, HALSALL, 1900

35868, HEYSHAM, VILLAGE 1895

35719, HOGHTON, TOWER 1895

18091, LANCASTER, TOWN HALL 1886

59132, LYTHAM, CLIFTON STREET 1907

42860, MORECAMBE, PROMENADE 1899

N146035, NELSON, MANCHESTER ROAD c1955

48579, ORMSKIRK, MOOR STREET 1902

50069, PRESTON, FISHERGATE 1903

71212, SLAIDBURN, CHURCH STREET 1921

53897, ST ANNE'S, ST ANNE'S ROAD 1906

42914, WADDINGTON, VILLAGE 1899

71116, WHALLEY, KING STREET 1921

40505, YEALAND, VILLAGE 1897

A212012, ASHBY DE LA ZOUCH, MARKET STREET c1955

27861, BELVOIR CASTLE, 1890

C432002, COALVILLE, BELVOIR ROAD 1956

E161003, EARL SHILTON, THE HOLLOW c1965

H266006, HINCKLEY, CASTLE STREET c1965

H358001, HOSE, POST OFFICE CORNER c1955

I48001, IBSTOCK, HIGH STREET c1965

L144015, LEICESTER, BELGRAVE GATE 1949

L197028, LOUGHBOROUGH, MARKET STREET c1955

L307005, LUTTERWORTH, CHURCH STREET c1955

72269, MARKET HARBOROUGH, OLD GRAMMAR SCHOOL 1922

M60031, MELTON MOWBRAY, NOTTINGHAM STREET c1955

80284, OAKHAM, HIGH STREET 1927

Q11009, QUORN, HIGH STREET c1965

85156, UPPINGHAM, MARKET PLACE AND CHURCH 1932

A209051, ALFORD, MARKET PLACE C1965

B536006, BINBROOK, MARKET PLACE C1955

43295, BOSTON, MARKET PLACE 1899

C427090, CHAPEL ST LEONARDS, THE VILLAGE C1955

C428013, COLSTERWORTH, THE VILLAGE C1960

C429013, CONINGSBY, HIGH STREET C1955

D150005, DEEPING ST JAMES, THE CROSS C1965

55116, DODDINGTON, VILLAGE 1906

D220015, DONINGTON, HIGH STREET C1955

G145008, GAINSBOROUGH, SILVER STREET C1955

51632, GRANTHAM, ST PETER'S HILL 1904

H63006, HECKINGTON, CHURCH STREET C1955

H316001, HEMSWELL, MAYPOLE STREET C1955

H318016, HOLBEACH, HIGH STREET C1955

H319030, HORNCASTLE, MARKET PLACE C1960

I47108, Ingoldmells, High Street c1965

55113, Lincoln, Stonebow 1906

L484011, Long Sutton, Market Place c1950

L305035, Louth, Mercer Row c1955

L509001, Ludford Magna, the Village c1955

26717, Mablethorpe, 1890

M116301, Market Deeping, 1900

M231013, Market Rasen, Market Place c1955

M232011, Metheringham, High Street c1955

N132008, Navenby, High Street c1965

N131013, North Somercotes, Village c1955

S479003, Saltfleet, High Street c1955

S480023, Sandilands, the Village c1955

S481010, Saxilby, High Street c1955

44354, Skegness, Lumley Road 1899

S482011, SKILLINGTON, THE VILLAGE c1965

S483029, SLEAFORD, MONUMENT c1950

S388171, SPALDING, MARKET PLACE c1955

S391028, SPILSBY, HIGH STREET c1955

72309, STAMFORD, ST MARY'S STREET 1922

S505003, SUTTERTON, STATION ROAD c1960

S235030, SUTTON ON SEA, HIGH STREET c1955

T15021, TATTERSHALL, THE GREEN c1955

T216013, TEALBY, THE VILLAGE c1960

T217010, TRUSTHORPE, THE POST OFFICE c1955

U41001, ULCEBY, HIGH STREET c1960

W550007, WAINFLEET ALL SAINTS, HIGH STREET c1955

W362010, WOODHALL SPA, BROADWAY c1965

W363006, WOOLSTHORPE, THE VILLAGE c1955

W382009, WRAGBY, MARKET PLACE c1965

Nostalgia is often derided as an emotion. Some critics have condemned it as a fruitless yearning for the past, leading to a reluctance to face the present and future. But what exactly is nostalgia? It is derived from two Greek words: *nostos* meaning return home, and *algos* meaning pain. Nostalgia means in its literal sense, homesickness. In former days nostalgia was the sickness afflicting young girls in service living away from their homes and families. It was said to be a cause of insomnia, heart palpitations and even insanity.

We are certainly not able to travel back in time, and many of us would not wish to. So can nostalgia - revisiting the people and places in our pasts - offer any real benefits to us in the modern world? Photographs have a strong, beneficial effect on our minds and emotions. They work on many levels in our psyches. Sending simple family 'snaps' of our children to our parents and grandparents can give them an opportunity to share in our daily lives. Seeing the places where we have lived and worked as they were twenty, fifty and a hundred years ago triggers differing levels of response and memory. It seems that rekindling pleasant memories can have a beneficial effect on our psyches. Old photographs recharge our mental and emotional batteries, helping us to regain spiritual strength to face the modern world once again.

We all know that suddenly hearing a line or two of a favourite song or catching a particular smell can evoke forgotten and very pleasurable memories. Memories have certainly been proved beneficial in helping the elderly. Therapists regularly use old photographs depicting holidays, schooldays and life and work to evoke memories in old people, stimulating their brains and encouraging them to communicate, thereby dispelling confusion in the present. Doctors confirm that the elderly react very positively to them, as memories are shared, and the past brought alive again.

Our family roots grow ever more vital to us in the modern world. On average we move house every five years, often because of our jobs, so that we no longer experience the continuity of life within a single community that our grandparents enjoyed. People find themselves in new towns and communities, that have a differing sense of place, and traditions that seem foreign compared to those to which they are accustomed.

Most of us have experienced returning to places we know and love and finding them almost unrecognisable: whole

roads have often disappeared, with new buildings smothering the fields and parks we played in as children. This is a reality of life we learn to take in our stride. The past is not a land of perfection, golden and without blemish, and most of us actually relish the challenges and opportunities that living in the modern world can offer. Yet we recognise, too, that life today can stretch family ties to the limit, our parents and relations often living counties apart in a way that was almost unknown a century ago. Taking time to enjoy old photographs can actively help us keep our bearings in a rapidly-changing world, by encouraging us to recall the places, buildings and people that were once a stable part of our everyday lives. The people who stare out at us from old photographs conjure a poignant reality, for they actually lived and existed. Unlike other forms of illustration, photographs are proofs of history, historical documents of unique authenticity, depicting real people and real moments in time.

Photographs make attractive additions to family history albums, offering a unique historical reality that engravings or drawings cannot achieve. An increasing number of people are involved in the assembly of such albums. Genealogy is one of the fastest growing of hobbies, and in America recent research indicates that 39% of the population have compiled a family tree. In Britain librarians confirm that a significant part of their time is taken up with dealing with genealogical enquiries. It is hardly surprising that more and more of us are enjoying and appreciating old photographs, recognising in them a valuable resource for family research and genealogy.

The places that hold meaning in our lives are many and various: the town or village where we were born, where we were christened, grew up, went to school, college and university, got married, and have lived since. We tend to lock away the past, because the demands of the present consume the bulk of our energies. We are consequently denied the benefits of well being that our memories can bestow on us. Our minds need to be jogged in order that we may recall the places in the past we have enjoyed. These grow in importance and significance as we ourselves grow older, as we begin the process of reflecting on the course of our lives. It is a sobering thought that every single one of the third of a million photographs in the Frith archive is special to someone. For each depicts a place intimately known, rich in personal association and significance.

Above: 44843 Shepton Mallet, Town Street 1899. Philip Hall's drapery shop, already established a full century before this photograph was taken.

A301007, ARDLEIGH GREEN, THE VILLAGE c1955

B10007, BALHAM, HIGH ROAD c1965

B440017, BARKING, EAST STREET c1955

B637001, BARKINGSIDE, HIGH ROAD c1955

B667001, BARNEHURST, c1955

B646032, BARNES, HIGH STREET c1955

B708016, BARNET, HIGH STREET 1940

44033, BATTERSEA, TOWN HALL 1899

43377, BECKENHAM, CHURCH HILL 1899

B50019, BEDDINGTON, CROYDON ROAD c1955

B654003, BEDFONT, STAINES ROAD c1955

B704004, BELVEDERE, ALBERT ROAD CORNER c1955

B83043, BEXLEY, HIGH STREET c1955

B650023, BEXLEYHEATH, WATLING STREET c1960

B400017, BRENTFORD, c1955

B666009, BRIXTON, STATION ROAD c1960

42935, BROMLEY, HIGH STREET 1899

B706007, BURNT OAK, EDGWARE ROAD c1955

37669, CARSHALTON, POND FROM THE BRIDGE 1896

C520010, CATFORD, THE GREEN MAN c1960

60608, CHADWELL HEATH, 1908

85087, CHEAM, THE BROADWAY 1932

58250, CHINGFORD, STATION ROAD 1907

C327032, CLAPHAM, HIGH STREET c1955

C580003, COLINDALE, EDGWARE ROAD c1955

57073, COULSDON, RED LION HOTEL 1906

C528004, CRAYFORD, CLOCK TOWER & BROADWAY c1965

C582006, CROUCH END, THE BROADWAY c1965

38651, CROYDON, NORTH END 1896

C207022, CRYSTAL PALACE, THE PAVILIONS 1900

D178004, DAGENHAM, CHURCH ELM LANE c1955

42658, DULWICH, TOLLGATE 1898

E63020, EALING, THE BROADWAY c1955

E198004, EARLS COURT, HIGH STREET c1965

E100003, EAST HAM, BARKING ROAD c1965

E178001, EASTCOTE, FIELD END ROAD c1965

E126031, EDGWARE, STATION ROAD c1955

E33069, ELTHAM, HIGH STREET AND ST. JOHN'S 1961

E179003, ENFIELD, MARKET PLACE c1955

E58012, ERITH, HIGH STREET c1955

F64039, FINCHLEY, HIGH ROAD c1955

45834, FOOTS CRAY, HIGH STREET 1900

42673, FOREST HILL, DEVONSHIRE ROAD 1898

F69001, FULHAM, BROADWAY 1890

G271009, GOLDERS GREEN, HIGH STREET c1955

G204010, Greenwich, College Promenade c1955

41570, Hampstead, High Street 1898

H369002, Hampton, c1955

43046, Hampton Court Palace, 1899

66820, Harrow on the Hill, Station Road 1914

H404021, Hatch End, the Broadway c1965

59847, Havering, Green 1908

H397022, Hendon, Vivian Avenue c1955

62081, Hornchurch, High Street 1909

H162012, Hounslow, High Street c1955

I59007, Ickenham, Glebe Avenue c1965

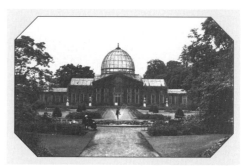

I35003, Isleworth, Syon House Orangery 1953

K9024, Kensington, High Street 1899

K151009, Kenton, High Street c1965

43760, Kew Gardens, 1899

K153014, Kilburn, High Road c1965

K142028, Kingsbury, Kingsbury Road c1960

31767, Kingston upon Thames, Coronation Stone 1893

L130139, Lambeth, Palace and Bridge c1900

L373013, Lewisham, High Street c1960

L374003, Leytonstone, High Road c1955

L130149, London, Houses of Parliament 1908

L130193, London, Royal Exchange c1910

70272, Malden, High Street 1921

M296030, Mitcham, Fair Green c1955

M279001, Mortlake, High Street c1955

M297010, Mottingham, Memorial c1965

M298365, Muswell Hill, 1910

N167009, New Malden, High Street c1955

42645, Norwood, Westow Hill 1898

O105004, Oakwood, the Station c1965

O107059, Orpington, High Street c1965

P295007, Palmers Green, Green Lanes c1965

P296030, Pinner, High Street c1965

49445, Purley, High Street 1903

P332010, Putney, High Street c1965

R355007, Raynes Park, High Street c1955

43739, Richmond, from Bridge 1899

59811, Romford, Market 1908

R335021, Ruislip, High Street c1955

S639006, Seven Kings, High Street c1955

S127060, Sidcup, the Oval c1955

S617011, South Ealing, c1955

S643006, South Woodford, High Road c1965

S641009, Southgate, Chase Side c1965

S647021, St Mary Cray, Marion Crescent c1955

55690, Stanmore, Village 1906

42785, Streatham, High Road 1898

S231022, Surbiton, Brighton Road c1955

85075, Sutton, High Street 1932

S650002, Swiss Cottage, Finchley Road c1965

42669, Sydenham, Hill 1898

T19024, Teddington, High Street c1960

T262007, Thornton Heath, High Street c1955

T263029, Tolworth, the Broadway c1965

T201006, Tooting, Mitcham Road c1955

T58015, Tooting Bec, the Common Pavilion c1955

T300343, Tottenham, Lordship Lane 1903

T91021, Twickenham, King Street c1955

60612, Upminster, the Market 1908

U52015, UXBRIDGE, HIGH STREET LOOKING EAST C1955

49185, WALLINGTON, MANOR ROAD 1903

55200, WALTHAMSTOW, ST JAMES STREET 1906

W21021, WANDSWORTH, HIGH STREET C1965

W22038, WANSTEAD, HIGH ROAD C1955

W281033, WELLING, WELLING CORNER C1955

W314018, WEMBLEY, HARROW ROAD C1960

W480016, WHETSTONE, HIGH ROAD C1955

W453008, WILLESDEN, HIGH ROAD C1965

W482001, WINCHMORE HILL, THE BROADWAY C1955

70105, WOODFORD, HIGH ROAD 1921

W479038, WOODFORD BRIDGE, HIGH ROAD C1965

70109, WOODFORD GREEN, SALWAY HILL 1921

W460024, WOOLWICH, MARKET 1963

W455041, WORCESTER PARK, CENTRAL ROAD C1960

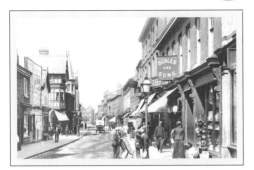

45448, Altrincham, George Street 1900

A137016, Ashton-in-Makerfield, Gerrard Street c1965

A138005, Atherton, Market Street c1955

B358009, Bamford, the Village c1955

35850, Bolton, Deansgate 1895

58602, Bowdon, Town Centre 1907

B360030, Bramhall, Bramhall Lane South c1960

36781, Bury, Market Street and Town Hall 1895

C284004, Chadderton, Library c1955

C536017, Cheadle, High Street c1960

C285022, Cheadle Hulme, Station Road c1955

D105010, Delph, King Street c1955

D84029, Denton, Manchester Road 1966

E88010, Eccles, Church Street c1960

F92001, Fallowfield, Princess Parade c1955

G126001, GATLEY, CHURCH ROAD C1955

58620, HALE, MAIN STREET 1907

H227017, HEATON MERSEY, DIDSBURY ROAD C1955

H228010, HEYWOOD, THE CENTRE C1955

L181004, LEIGH, BRADSHAWGATE C1955

22159, MANCHESTER, PICCADILLY 1889

O39002, OLDHAM, HIGH STREET 1951

65599, ROCHDALE, TOWN HALL SQUARE 1913

R255018, ROMILEY, COMSTALL ROAD C1960

S344001, SALE, NORTHENDEN ROAD C1955

T144002, TOTTINGTON, MARKET STREET C1955

T145004, TYLDESLEY, ELLIOTT STREET 1950

W250001, WESTHOUGHTON, MARKET STREET C1955

W98004, WIGAN, THE MARKET PLACE C1955

22262, WORSLEY, CANAL 1889

A174035, Ainsdale, Station Road c1965

B441003, Barnston, The Fox and Hounds c1955

B660013, Bebington, Bebington Road c1965

B399006, Birkenhead, Crossroads 1954

B444013, Blundellsands, Bridge Road c1960

B445034, Bromborough, Allport Lane c1965

C356004, Caldy, the Village c1955

C714044, Churchtown, Botanic Road c1955

C357009, Crosby, Myers Road East c1965

E218005, Earlestown, Market Street c1960

E90007, Eastham, the Village c1955

48662, Egremont, Promenade 1912

F106005, Formby, Chapel Lane 1957

F117003, Freshfield, Cores Lane c1965

M191027, Great Meols, Station Approach c1955

H276051, HESWALL, THE VILLAGE c1955

H277019, HOYLAKE, MARKET STREET c1955

I42005, IRBY, THE VILLAGE c1955

L233010, LEASOWE, CASTLE c1965

26661, LIVERPOOL, LIME STREET 1890

M192016, MORETON, COACH AND HORSES c1965

45163, NEW BRIGHTON, TOWER AND SANDS 1900

N149004, NEWTON-LE-WILLOWS, HIGH STREET c1955

P188071, PORT SUNLIGHT, THE POST OFFICE c1960

35617, POULTON, MARKET PLACE 1895

75767, SOUTHPORT, NEVILLE STREET 1924

S415023, ST HELENS, ORMSKIRK STREET c1965

U36002, UPTON, THE VILLAGE c1955

W164006, WALLASEY, THE VILLAGE c1955

W170049, WEST KIRBY, THE CRESCENT 1967

A204004, ACLE, THE GREEN FROM THE POST OFFICE c1926

A278003, ALDBOROUGH, THE BLACK BOYS c1955

A227002, ANCHORSHOLME, MAGDALEN ROAD c1955

A220047, AYLSHAM, MARKET PLACE c1965

B493011, BACTON, c1955

B494012, BANHAM, THE GREEN c1965

B121050, BLAKENEY, MAIN STREET c1955

B321010, BRADFIELD, c1955

B301004, BRAMERTON, 1953

B401008, BRANCASTER, LONDON STREET c1965

B541001, BROOKE, THE POST OFFICE c1955

B501001, BURNHAM NORTON, c1955

C450004, CAISTER-ON-SEA, THE RAILWAY STATION c1955

C41021, CASTLE ACRE, THE VILLAGE c1955

C45016, CASTLE RISING, TRINITY HOSPITAL c1955

C415010, CAWSTON, HIGH STREET c1965

C118013, CLEY NEXT THE SEA, HIGH STREET c1955

C417027, COLTISHALL, THE VILLAGE c1955

49071, CROMER, CHURCH STREET 1902

D148014, DERSINGHAM, HUNSTANTON ROAD c1965

77322, DISS, MARKET PLACE 1925

D149033, DOWNHAM MARKET, BRIDGE STREET c1965

72556, EAST DEREHAM, JUBILEE ROAD 1922

E132010, EAST HARLING, HIGH STREET c1965

E11052, EAST RUNTON, HIGH STREET c1955

F3002, FAKENHAM, NORWICH STREET c1955

G188019, GARBOLDISHAM, VILLAGE c1955

G189020, GAYWOOD, THE CLOCK TOWER c1965

G298004, GIMINGHAM, MILL STREET c1955

G209161, GLANDFORD, THE FORD AND CHURCH c1965

60663, GORLESTON, HIGH STREET 1908

G192001, GREAT HOCKHAM, THE VILLAGE C1955

G193006, GREAT HOLLAND, C1955

G210005, GREAT MASSINGHAM, THE VILLAGE C1955

37957, GREAT YARMOUTH, KINGS STREET 1896

H305001, HARLESTON, THE MARKET PLACE C1955

71046, HEACHAM, HIGH STREET 1921

H306300, HEMSBY, THE VILLAGE C1955

H395025, HICKLING BROAD, C1955

H307011, HICKLING GREEN, PLEASURE BOAT INN C1955

H308004, HILGAY, BRIDGE STREET C1955

H309011, HINGHAM, THE MARKET PLACE C1955

H340002, HOLKHAM, THE VILLAGE STORES C1955

72640, HOLKHAM HALL, 1922

37976, HOLT, HIGH STREET 1896

H310052, HOPTON, LONDON ROAD c1960

86365, HORNING, VILLAGE 1934

H341005, HORSEY, THE VILLAGE c1955

H342006, HORSHAM ST FAITH, MAIN ROAD c1960

58898, HUNSTANTON, HIGH STREET 1907

60024, KINGS LYNN, HIGH STREET 1908

L369017, LODDON, OLD SCHOOL c1965

L300001, LONG STRATTON, THE VILLAGE c1965

L110030, LUDHAM, THE VILLAGE c1960

M228019, MARTHAM, THE POND c1955

M59009, MELTON CONSTABLE, THE VILLAGE c1955

M229007, METHWOLD, HIGH STREET c1960

M248064, MORSTON, THE VILLAGE c1955

71010, MUNDESLEY, HIGH STREET 1921

N189019, NARBOROUGH, THE VILLAGE c1955

70936, NORTH WALSHAM, MARKET PLACE 1921

28163, NORWICH, RAMPART HORSE STREET 1891

O119103, OLD HUNSTANTON, THE CHURCH c1955

O31108, OVERSTRAND, MAIN STREET c1965

O80004, OVERY STAITHE, THE VILLAGE c1955

R304022, REEPHAM, MARKET PLACE c1965

S507017, SALTHOUSE, CROSS STREET c1955

S508002, SCOLE, THE VILLAGE c1955

S470005, SEA PALLING, THE VILLAGE c1955

S513009, SEDGEFORD, THE VILLAGE c1960

46544, SHERINGHAM, HIGH STREET 1901

S464006, SNETTISHAM, THE VILLAGE c1955

S467004, STALHAM, c1955

S193012, STIFFKEY, POST OFFICE CORNER c1955

S469047, STOKESBY, THE VILLAGE c1965

Norfolk

S472003, SUDBURY, MARKET HILL AND ST PETER'S c1955

29104, SWAFFHAM, MARKET PLACE 1891

T225012, TEN MILE BANK, STATION ROAD c1955

T213064, THE BROADS, MILL AND RIVER c1934

70915, THETFORD, ST CUTHBERT'S CHURCH 1921

T250002, THORPE ST ANDREW, HIGH STREET c1955

72626, WALSINGHAM, MARKET PLACE 1922

W383004, WATTON, HIGH STREET c1955

81996, WELLS-NEXT-THE-SEA, 1929

W338012, WEST DEREHAM, CHEQUERS & POST OFFICE c1955

74219, WEST RUNTON, 1923

W353005, WEYBOURNE, HIGH STREET c1955

W357077, WINTERTON-ON-SEA, BEACH ROAD c1955

70890, WROXHAM, VILLAGE 1921

W159017, WYMONDHAM, MARKET STREET c1955

A298020, ABINGTON, HIGH STREET c1955

B283001, BLISWORTH, VILLAGE c1955

B701002, BOZEAT, RED LION c1955

B698004, BRACKLEY, HIGH STREET c1955

B778004, BRAUNSTON, HIGH STREET c1955

B390006, BURTON LATIMER, HIGH STREET c1955

B703004, BYFIELD, HIGH STREET c1955

C337015, CORBY, STATION ROAD c1955

D83064, DAVENTRY, HIGH STREET c1965

D200033, DESBOROUGH, HIGH STREET c1960

E97027, EARLS BARTON, SQUARE c1965

72253, GEDDINGTON, VILLAGE 1922

72214, GREAT BRINGTON, POST OFFICE 1922

G137007, GREAT DODDINGTON, HIGH STREET c1965

G223008, GREAT HOUGHTON, HIGH STREET c1965

H418310, Hardingstone, High Street c1955

H245028, Higham Ferrers, Market Square c1965

I71006, Irchester, High Street c1955

I33020, Irthingborough, High Street 1969

72232, Kettering, Market 1922

M294009, Milton Malsor, High Street c1955

M295007, Moulton, High Street c1955

72171, Northampton, Abington Street 1922

O103033, Oundle, Market Place c1955

R82017, Raunds, High Street c1955

R223030, Rushden, High Street c1965

T104008, Thrapston, High Street 1951

W279024, Wellingborough, Midland Road c1955

W421014, Wollaston, High Street c1955

Y42005, Yardley Gobion, High Street c1965

A223017, ALNWICK, BONDGATE & MARKET PLACE c1955

A225038, AMBLE, QUEEN STREET c1960

B547022, BAMBURGH, VILLAGE AND CASTLE c1955

B551007, BEDLINGTON, THE MARKET PLACE c1955

B553071, BELFORD, THE SQUARE c1955

B552046, BELLINGHAM, MARKET PLACE c1960

B305035, BERWICK-UPON-TWEED, THE BORDER BRIDGE 1954

B555062, BLANCHLAND, THE SQUARE c1955

E150043, EMBLETON, FRONT STREET c1960

H344046, HALTWHISTLE, MAIN STREET c1960

H80095, HEXHAM, BEAUMONT STREET c1965

M251059, MORPETH, BRIDGE STREET c1965

R360047, ROTHBURY, c1955

S521135, SEAHOUSES, THE HARBOUR c1965

W396057, WOOLER, MARKET SQUARE c1955

The sheer clarity of detail and broad tonal range of Frith's vintage sepia photographic prints is remarkable. Their quality has never been surpassed, even with the most modern photographic emulsions. The processes involved in creating them were many and painstaking.

Frith's glass plate negatives were the equivalent of our modern-day roll films. A sheet of glass was coated with a film of collodion, which was a mixture of gun-cotton dissolved in ether, sensitised with silver nitrate. These were known as 'wet plates'. Taking the photograph was not a simple affair. The 'wet plate' was inserted into the bulky brass camera and the exposure made by removing the lens cap. Exposure times were long - up to a full minute. These long exposure times are the reason why some old photographs feature blurred figures, shifting eerily across the scene. They were simply moving too fast for the emulsion to capture.

This Victorian woodtype illustration depicts a photographer in his studio, examining a glass plate negative he has just coated with collodion

Once exposed, the glass plate negative had to be developed almost immediately. Early glass negatives produced prints of remarkable clarity and detail and with a broad tonal range. The thin paper employed for making prints was coated with a very fine film of egg-white (albumen) and salt, then sensitised with silver nitrate. The printing process was not one that we would recognise today, for no enlarger nor dark-room was involved. A sheet of albumen paper was placed in direct contact with the glass plate and left in daylight for up to an hour. After fixing, the result was a print with a distinctly rich reddish-brown tone. Some of Frith's prints were toned again with a gold solution, which reduced the likelihood of fading.

It will be clear that 'wet plate' negatives were both inconvenient and cumbersome, requiring the carrying around of sensitive chemicals and prompt development. In 1878 gelatine 'dry plate' negatives went into general manufacture, and these were in use in the Frith & Co archive up until the 1940s, when film negatives gradually superseded glass.

Frith's glass plates presented him with a formidable storage problem, for they needed to be carefully stowed well away from light, dust and the dangers of accidental damage. This was no small task - for in 1970, when the archive was purchased by Rothman's, there was still a legacy remaining of eleven tons of glass. Many plates, unfortunately, did not survive, and examples have been found serving as cloches in vegetable beds!

In contrast to all this, the Frith archive today has the very latest in digital computer technology at its disposal, and Francis Frith's complex and space-hungry Victorian storage problem has been converted into a matter of a few cabinets of compact disks. Creating a finished print is now a less laborious affair. Each Victorian original photograph can be 'read' in seconds by a computer scanner which converts it instantly into digital computer language. The picture can then be called up onto a monitor screen, titled and dated via the keyboard and printed out in a variety of sizes and forms.

Digitised images are increasingly stored in powerful computer database programmes. Operators are now able to sort many thousands of images into a wide variety of classifications much more readily than was ever the case in Frith's time. This new technology offers particular benefits for social and historical studies. Researchers can now access relevant material in a fraction of the time it would take to carry out manual searches.

Frith & Co employed one device to prolong the useful life of its images, retouching. Some original prints, still held in the archive today, show artists' retouching work, especially to items such as costume and dress that can clearly date a view. Using sepia watercolour tones, these features were carefully painted out and subtle additions and alterations made. These personal touches bring us a curious empathy with all the many men and women who worked with Francis Frith down the years, and add a fascinating insight into the history of the archive and its working practices.

Today, photographs can be manipulated on the computer to an extraordinary degree. Tears in the paper can be 'rubbed out' and other marks and blemishes corrected.

The present owners of the archive are certain that Francis Frith, whose eye was always on the future and on the potential of Victorian technology, would be fascinated and gratified to see what is being continued today in his name. It would surely astonish him to see a book such as this, illustrated with over 2,000 of his photographs, created and assembled electronically. It would please him, too, that his photographs are as avidly sought after today as they were in his own time. Their useful life has been extended far beyond his wildest dreams. His pictures are still being purchased today by people all over the country as mementoes of favourite towns and villages but, in addition, the archive has become an essential tool for reference libraries, humanities departments, genealogists and picture researchers.

61814, BALDERTON, THE VILLAGE 1909

B651005, BINGHAM, MARKET STREET C1955

61827, CARLTON-ON-TRENT, THE VILLAGE 1909

E183004, EASTWOOD, NOTTINGHAM ROAD C1955

H373017, HUCKNALL, HIGH STREET C1965

M184013, MANSFIELD, TOOTHILL LANE 1949

M235044, MISTERTON, STATION STREET C1955

56498, NEWARK-ON-TRENT, APPLETON GATE 1906

22856, NEWSTEAD ABBEY, 1890

48327, NOTTINGHAM, WHEELER GATE 1902

R261030, RETFORD, MARKET PLACE C1955

69472, SOUTHWELL, KING STREET 1920

66085, SUTTON ON TRENT, CHURCH STREET 1913

24681, THURGARTON, PRIORY 1890

W278084, WORKSOP, BRIDGE STREET MARKET C1965

26994, Abingdon, Market Place 1890

A139001, Adderbury, High Street c1955

70572, Banbury, Market Place 1921

B364049, Benson, High Street c1965

K365001, Bicester, Market Square c1955

B367008, Bloxham, Old Bridge Road c1955

B369011, Burford, High Street c1955

C288037, Chipping Norton, High Street c1955

27010, Clifton Hampden, The Barley Mow Inn 1890

D108041, Didcot, Broadway 1950

27015, Dorchester, Village 1890

E92008, Eynsham, High Street c1965

F94021, Faringdon, c1955

42991, Goring, Village 1899

G130017, Great Tew, Stocks c1960

31732, HENLEY-ON-THAMES, MARKET PLACE 1893

26959, IFFLEY, THE MILL LOCK AND BRIDGE 1890

27091, MAPLEDURHAM, THE MILL 1890

26969, NUNEHAM COURTENAY, OXFORD STEAMER 1890

71994, OXFORD, CORNMARKET STREET 1922

27018, SHILLINGFORD, SWAN HOTEL 1890

27167, SHIPLAKE, MILL AND LOCK 1890

27001, SUTTON COURTENAY, VILLAGE 1890

T106011, THAME, CORN MARKET 1951

31712, WALLINGFORD, MARKET PLACE 1893

W251011, WANTAGE, THE SQUARE AND TOWN HALL c1955

W254023, WATLINGTON, TOWN HALL c1955

43002, WHITCHURCH, ROYAL OAK 1899

W256017, WITNEY, THE MARKET SQUARE c1955

W258019, WOODSTOCK, OXFORD STREET 1950

38126A, BRIDGNORTH, HIGH STREET 1896

30842, BROMFIELD, MILL AND CHURCH 1892

51385, BROSELEY, HIGH STREET 1904

62721, CHURCH STRETTON, HIGH STREET 1910

C506030, CLEOBURY MORTIMER, CHURCH STREET c1955

D169009, DAWLEY, HIGH STREET c1955

76923, IRONBRIDGE, 1925

87393, LUDLOW, BROAD STREET AND ANGEL HOTEL 1936

63338, MARKET DRAYTON, MARKET DAY 1911

63261, MUCH WENLOCK, GASKELL ARMS 1911

41982, NEWPORT, HIGH STREET 1893

44139, OAKENGATES, MARKET STREET 1899

44150, SHIFNAL, MARKET PLACE 1899

83877, SHREWSBURY, HIGH STREET 1931

51130, WELLINGTON, CHURCH STREET 1903

64872, ALCOMBE, THE VILLAGE 1912

45703, ALLERFORD, BRIDGE 1900

A254058, AXBRIDGE, THE SQUARE c1955

87562, BLUE ANCHOR, THE VILLAGE 1936

84861, BOSSINGTON, THE VILLAGE 1931

65392, BRENT KNOLL, THE VILLAGE 1913

27899, BRIDGWATER, MARKET AND CHURCH 1890

79282, BURNHAM-ON-SEA, THE PARADE 1926

58762, CHARD, FORE STREET 1907

60145, CHEDDAR, 1908

C185031, CREWKERNE, MARKET SQUARE c1955

37653, DULVERTON, LION HOTEL 1896

15837, DUNSTER, MARKET HOUSE AND CASTLE c1880

61542, GLASTONBURY, HIGH STREET 1909

58742, ILMINSTER, WEST STREET 1907

L365008, LANGPORT, CHEAPSIDE c1955

80615, MINEHEAD, THE PARADE 1927

23512, PORLOCK, HIGH STREET 1890

83518, ROADWATER, THE VILLAGE 1930

15836, SELWORTHY, 1883

44843, SHEPTON MALLET, TOWN STREET 1899

55814, SOMERTON, TOWN HALL 1906

38386, STREET, 1896

78808, TAUNTON, HIGH STREET 1925

65343, WASHFORD, 1913

56800, WATCHET, SWAIN STREET 1906

88415, WELLINGTON, FORE STREET 1938

73991, WELLS, MARKET PLACE 1923

82098, WILLITON, LONG STREET 1929

49166, YEOVIL, MIDDLE STREET 1903

A165007, Abbots Bromley, High Street c1955

A318010, Alrewas, the Village c1965

A284011, Alstonefield, the Village c1955

A285008, Alton, Lower Village c1955

B611015, Biddulph, High Street c1955

B680016, Brewood, Market Square c1965

B286016, Burton upon Trent, Station Street c1960

C691003, Caverswall, the Village c1955

D191023, Denstone, the Village c1965

46157, Eccleshall, High Street 1900

44333, Gnosall, Village 1899

G232001, Golden Hill, High Street c1955

G303007, Great Haywood, the Square c1955

H334006, Hanley, Town Road c1965

H267306, Hednesford, Market Street c1955

84702, KINVER, HIGH STREET 1931

L379003, LEEK, MARKET PLACE c1955

L45055, LICHFIELD, BIRD STREET c1955

L312002, LITTLE HAYWOOD, HIGH STREET c1955

M292004, MARCHINGTON, HIGH STREET c1955

N93005, NEWCASTLE UNDER LYME, HIGH STREET 1951

R271004, RUGELEY, THE MARKET PLACE 1951

S411010, STAFFORD, ANCIENT HIGH HOUSE 1948

46171, STONE, HIGH STREET 1900

46206, SWYNNERTON, THE VILLAGE 1900

T157002, TAMWORTH, MARKET STREET c1955

T88016, TUNSTALL, TOWN HALL c1955

U29015, UTTOXETER, MARKET PLACE c1955

W323018, WOMBOURN, HIGH STREET c1965

Y41011, YOXALL, VICTORIA STREET c1955

62009, ALDEBURGH, HIGH STREET 1909

78286, BARTON MILLS, 1925

34807, BAWDSEY, 1894

33335, BECCLES, MARKET PLACE 1894

B766021, BILDESTON, THE SQUARE C1960

36881, BLYTHBURGH, CHURCH AND VILLAGE 1895

78266, BRANDON, HIGH STREET 1925

B617026, BUNGAY, MARKET PLACE 1951

41246, BURY ST EDMUNDS, MARKET PLACE 1898

62043, DUNWICH, VILLAGE 1909

44513, FELIXSTOWE, FROM THE BEACH 1899

82062, FRAMLINGHAM, MARKET HILL 1929

H2007, HADLEIGH, HIGH STREET C1955

H384019, HALESWORTH, MARKET PLACE C1955

32204, IPSWICH, BUTTER MARKET 1893

51180, Lavenham, 1904

37924, Lowestoft, London Road 1896

78280, Mildenhall, Mill Street 1925

71933, Needham Market, High Street 1922

81955, Newmarket, High Street 1929

020065, Orford, the Village c1955

82946, Saxmundham, 1929

38627, Southwold, Market 1896

S583007, Stowmarket, Ipswich Street c1955

51157, Sudbury, Market 1904

82989, Thorpeness, 1929

69128, Walberswick, Village 1919

82046, Wickham Market, Market Hill 1929

60685, Woodbridge, Town Hall 1908

62051, Yoxford, Village 1909

76846, ABINGER, HATCH HOTEL 1925

81469, ABINGER HAMMER, 1928

A219048, ADDINGTON, THE VILLAGE c1965

51707, ADDLESTONE, STATION ROAD 1904

A302033, ALFOLD, THE VILLAGE c1950

69970, ASH VALE, THE VILLAGE 1921

52583, ASHTEAD, 1904

50983, BAGSHOT, HIGH STREET 1903

B391007, BANSTEAD, HIGH STREET 1950

B720021, BEACON HILL, THE VILLAGE c1965

61665, BEARE GREEN, VILLAGE SHOP 1909

45010, BETCHWORTH, 1900

B109027, BISLEY, THE VILLAGE c1955

53383, BLACKHEATH, THE VILLAGE 1906

50839, BLETCHINGLEY, VILLAGE 1903

B123016, BLINDLEY HEATH, THE VILLAGE c1955

51892, BRAMLEY, HIGH STREET 1904

55137, BROCKHAM, THE VILLAGE 1906

B230006, BROOK, THE DOG AND PHEASANT c1955

B232012, BROOKWOOD, CONNAUGHT ROAD c1955

B265055, BYFLEET, HIGH STREET c1965

79600, CAMBERLEY, HIGH STREET 1927

80773, CAPEL, POST OFFICE AND VILLAGE 1928

78134, CATERHAM, 1925

52386, CHARLWOOD, 1904

60929, CHERTSEY, GUILDFORD STREET 1908

48362, CHIDDINGFOLD, VILLAGE AND POND 1902

C395008, CHOBHAM, HIGH STREET c1955

85392, CHURT, POST OFFICE 1932

55642, CLANDON, VILLAGE 1906

84918, COBHAM, HIGH STREET 1932

67763, COLDHARBOUR, THE VILLAGE 1915

52440, COMPTON, THE WITHIES 1904

51303, CRANLEIGH, ROWLANDS CORNER 1904

71736, DORKING, HIGH STREET 1922

41806, EASHING, VILLAGE 1898

38350, EAST MOLESEY, HOUSEBOATS IN LOCK 1896

E27015, EGHAM, HIGH STREET c1955

55623, ELSTEAD, 1906

75368, EPSOM, HIGH STREET 1924

E64023, ESHER, HIGH STREET c1955

75489, EWELL, HIGH STREET 1924

72083, EWHURST, 1922

57613, FARNCOMBE, HIGH STREET 1907

75293, FARNHAM, THE BOROUGH 1924

77153, FELBRIDGE, 1925

F47077, FRENSHAM, MILLBRIDGE c1965

81637, FRIDAY STREET, RIVER AND VILLAGE 1929

69920, FRIMLEY, HIGH STREET 1921

59650, FRIMLEY GREEN, 1908

54163, GODALMING, HIGH STREET 1906

53288, GODSTONE, HIGH STREET 1905

48358, GRAYSWOOD, VILLAGE 1902

51515A, GREAT BOOKHAM, LOWER STREET 1904

73379, GUILDFORD, HIGH STREET 1923

H14025, HAMBLEDON, HIGH STREET c1965

53577, HASCOMBE, WHITE HOUSE 1906

79521, HASLEMERE, HIGH STREET 1927

H61025, HEADLEY, HIGH STREET c1955

75207, HINDHEAD, POST OFFICE CORNER 1924

53387, HOLMBURY ST MARY, THE GREEN 1906

86774, HURTMORE, FARM 1935

63137, KNAPHILL, HIGH STREET 1911

66112, LEATHERHEAD, HIGH STREET 1913

54268, LEIGH, 1906

57062, LIMPSFIELD, VILLAGE 1906

52986, LINGFIELD, THE STAR COMMERCIAL HOTEL 1904

71750, LITTLE BOOKHAM, YE OLDE WINDSOR CASTLE 1922

53404, MEADVALE, SOMERSET ROAD 1906

65231, MERROW, THE FORGE 1913

49091, MERSTHAM, 1902

75521, NEWDIGATE, SIX BELLS 1924

53525, OCKLEY, 1906

51788, OXSHOTT, VILLAGE 1904

59615, OXTED, HIGH STREET 1908

50274, PEASLAKE, VILLAGE 1903

59655, PIRBRIGHT, THE WHITE HART 1908

55035, REDHILL, HIGH STREET 1906

85475, REIGATE, HIGH STREET 1933

55353, RIPLEY, 1906

68351, ROWLEDGE, THE SQUARE 1918

57625, SALFORDS, 1907

55629, SEALE, VILLAGE 1906

57602, SHACKLEFORD, CYDER HOUSE AND LANE 1907

51877, SHALFORD, VILLAGE 1904

53615, SHAMLEY GREEN, CHURCH 1906

50269, SHERE, THE VILLAGE 1903

57995, STAINES, HIGH STREET 1907

S588002, STANWELL, HIGH STREET C1955

51789, STOKE D'ABERNON, 1904

61134, Stoughton, High Street 1908

T103011, Thames Ditton, c1955

57522, Thursley, The Red Lion 1907

53597, Tongham, Village 1906

84417, Walton on the Hill, Post Office 1931

50586, Walton-on-Thames, Bridge Street 1903

W456023, West Byfleet, Station Approach c1955

54693, West Humble, 1906

71741, Westcott, 1922

55657, Weybridge, High Street 1906

W93035, Whyteleafe, High Street c1960

46342, Woking, Albion Hotel 1901

W127002, Wonersh, the Village c1955

51901, Worplesdon, 1904

56335, Wrecclesham, Village 1907

Every Frith picture has strong personal associations for someone. Yet each, too, has a more general story to tell. Here are two very different examples, reflecting the essence of both city and country life in days gone by.

Pooter's World - The Victorian Yuppie

The heart of the Square Mile in 1897: the Royal Exchange with Threadneedle Street behind.
Victorian city life looks just as frantic as today. The bowler-hatted gent in the foreground is dashing from the Bank of England to his office with the latest figures (there were no fax machines in Victoria's day). And judging by the packed top deck on the left, there were never enough London buses to go around to keep commuters on the move.
How could you better yourself in the City a hundred years ago? If you were bright and hard-working, they might make you a senior clerk after many years of loyal service. Job mobility was unheard of in the Victorian office, and staying with the same employer was your only chance of security and receiving a modest pension. You'd try hard to find a post in a bank or insurance office because they paid the best salary. Law offices were the meanest. You would start at seven, and if you complained about the poor light or the bad air you would not get very far: even the union failed to improve working conditions. The best way up the ladder was to specialise and become a ledger or billing clerk. But you had to watch your back: young women were taking over the office desks, and typing pools were being set up (the typewriter first appeared in the 1880s).

L130055 London, Queen Victoria Street 1897

So how different was city life a century ago for the ordinary office worker? George Pooter, that quintessentially ordinary man, gives us a crystal clear picture in 'Diary of a Nobody', written in 1892. He proudly reported to his wayward son, Lupin: *'My boy, after 21 years of industry and strict attention to the interests of my superiors, I have been rewarded with the position of Senior Clerk and a salary increase of £100.'* Unimpressed, Lupin informed his father that after five days in his new job, and with no attention whatsoever to the interests of his superiors, he had made £200. How? On a risky share deal.
Nothing, it seems, has changed. Except that thousands of George Pooters have been replaced by IBMs, which, of course, have an even greater, if more slavish, loyalty to their employer than George Pooter.

An Eye for a Bargain at Barnstaple Pannier Market

A sea of hats and upturned faces. Business at the Barnstaple Pannier Market has been suspended for a few precious moments for the Frith & Co photographer. As soon as he steps down from his viewing platform we can be sure the bargaining will begin again in earnest. Everyone in

69324 Barnstaple, Pannier Market 1919

Devon seems to have turned out. Even the curate is there in the thick of it, searching for his favourite chutney.
Barnstaple Pannier Market was built in 1855. Its wooden vaulted roof is roomy and cathedral-like, exalting the proceedings below. On the fringes of the crowd stand the stall holders, including farmers and their wives, country women and old men. For most the few pence earned were a vital part of their weekly household budget, but for others the sale of a few vegetables helped pay the cost of tobacco.
A woman in white stands on the left by her pannier basket. She was up before dawn, filling it with jars of jam and marmalade, fresh-picked cabbages and cucumbers. Then she had the long journey on the local carrier's cart through the twisting Devon lanes into town.
Inside the huge market building each stall holder had a numbered pitch. The baskets went on the floor and the trader flopped down on to a bench for a well-earned rest before the doors were flung open. The cost of a year's rent? 6d. Today it is eighty pounds or more, and still considered a bargain. On Tuesdays, Fridays and Saturdays you can pick over the produce of 400 stalls. Prices are low and you will see items not to be found in the high street shops, like cottage garden plants and forgotten varieties of apple. You may even spot the last pannier basket still in use - everyone else these days uses tables.

71422, Alfriston, High Street 1921

A327036, Angmering-on-Sea, The Village c1955

A207017, Ardingly, The Village c1955

48792, Arundel, High Street 1902

A263006, Ashurstwood, Maypole Road c1955

71507, Battle, High Street 1921

50317, Bexhill, Old Town 1903

62165, Billingshurst, High Street 1909

B128015, Bodiam, The Village c1965

66933, Bognor Regis, High Street 1914

B152009, Bosham, High Street c1955

B179002, Bramber, The Village c1955

71498, Brighton, The Aquarium 1921

56718, Broadwater, Village 1906

B284002, Burgess Hill, Station Approach 1950

54367, BYWORTH, THE VILLAGE 1906

C532009, CATSFIELD, THE VILLAGE C1955

C437013, CHAILEY, VILLAGE C1965

22618, CHICHESTER, MARKET CROSS 1890

54385, COCKING, THE VILLAGE 1906

C424006, COOLHAM, POST OFFICE AND STORE C1955

53326, CRAWLEY, FAIR 1905

44935, CROWBOROUGH, CROSS 1900

C426022, CUCKFIELD, HIGH STREET C1965

E136060, EAST DEAN, VILLAGE GREEN C1955

66751, EAST GRINSTEAD, LONDON ROAD 1914

83452, EAST WITTERING, BEACH 1930

77946, EASTBOURNE, THE PIER 1925

F136008, FAIRWARP, THE VILLAGE C1955

82452, FAYGATE, HORSHAM ROAD 1929

59672, FERNHURST, 1908

70081, FITTLEWORTH, UPPER STREET 1921

F40011, FOREST ROW, THE VILLAGE C1955

F139014, FRAMFIELD, C1955

F173010, FRANT, THE VILLAGE C1955

G194044, GORING-BY-SEA, PARADE C1960

G195006, GRAFFHAM, THE VILLAGE C1955

44957, HAILSHAM, GEORGE STREET 1899

H327002, HALLAND, THE VILLAGE C1955

H311045, HANDCROSS, RED LION HOTEL C1965

H28006, HARTFIELD, HIGH STREET C1965

H360003, HARTING, HIGH STREET C1955

77975, HASTINGS, VIEW FROM PIER 1925

H252012, HAYWARDS HEATH, SOUTH ROAD 1954

H313058, HENFIELD, HIGH STREET C1965

H329039, HORAM, HIGH STREET c1955

53298, HORLEY, STATION ROAD 1905

85574, HORSHAM, THE CARFAX 1933

41896, HOVE, CHURCH ROAD 1898

53330, IFIELD, 1905

L11006, LANCING, NORTH STREET c1955

50924, LEWES, HIGH STREET 1903

L368003, LITTLE COMMON, WHEATSHEAF INN c1960

29970, LITTLEHAMPTON, HIGH STREET 1892

M242022, MAYFIELD, HIGH STREET c1955

70084, MIDHURST, NORTH STREET 1921

27760, NEWHAVEN, HIGH STREET 1890

N90016, NEWICK, THE GREEN c1955

48368, NORTHCHAPEL, VILLAGE 1902

80745, NUTLEY, POST OFFICE 1928

O81018, Offham, the Village c1960

P257004, Peasmarsh, High Street c1955

54362, Petworth, East Street 1906

P50085, Pevensey, the Village c1965

P259025, Polegate, High Street c1955

88912, Pulborough, the Village 1939

37139, Rottingdean, 1896

R305009, Rudgwick, the King's Head c1955

61379, Rusper, Village 1909

R81000, Rustington, Sea Lane 1906

47444, Rye, from Church 1901

45120, Seaford, Church Street 1900

S91019, Selsey, High Street c1955

69000, Shoreham, Bridge 1919

29605, St Leonards, from Boundary 1891

67059, Steyning, 1914

S210086, Storrington, High Street c1960

53309, Three Bridges, 1905

49352, Ticehurst, Village and Church 1903

48198, Uckfield, High Street 1902

U40002, Upper Beeding, from Bridge c1955

64900, Upperton, the Village 1912

49366, Wadhurst, High Street 1903

W359025, Washington, the Village c1960

W360007, West Chiltington, Crossroads c1955

35226, West Hoathly, 1895

W325008, West Wittering, Village Green c1960

64941, Winchelsea, Barrack Square 1912

38176, Wisborough Green, 1896

43956, Worthing, South Street 1899

B357031, BIRTLEY, DURHAM ROAD C1965

G124001, GATESHEAD, SALTWELL PARK LAKE C1955

G125008, GOSFORTH, HIGH STREET 1956

H225006, HOUGHTON-LE-SPRING, THE BROADWAY C1955

J5004, JARROW, GRANGE ROAD WEST C1955

N59001, NEWBURN, STATION ROAD 1951

N16016, NEWCASTLE UPON TYNE, QUAYSIDE 1928

R252009, RYHOPE, RYHOPE ROAD C1960

S162003, SOUTH SHIELDS, KING STREET 1905

S263001, SUNDERLAND, FAWCETT STREET 1890

W168001, WALLSEND, HIGH STREET C1955

W242010, WASHINGTON, FRONT STREET C1955

W244001, WHICKHAM, FRONT STREET C1955

W246002, WHITLEY BAY, PLEASURE GARDENS C1955

W248011, WINLATON, THE VILLAGE C1955

B91075, Bidford-on-Avon, High Street c1955

72072, Edge Hill, Round Tower 1922

H414027, Henley-in-Arden, Market Square c1955

72405, Kenilworth, Castle 1922

K65019, Kineton, Boutham Street c1965

30961, Leamington, Parish Church 1892

L166007, Long Itchington, Village c1955

N89401, Nuneaton, c1960

P64012, Polesworth, Market Square 1958

72125, Rugby, Clock Tower & St Andrew's 1922

72399, Shottery, the Village 1922

31073, Stratford-on-Avon, Market Place 1892

U19004, Ullenhall, Village c1955

72345, Warwick, Church Street 1922

72483, Whitnash, Village 1922

A136014, Acocks Green, Yardley Road c1965

B353004, Bilston, c1960

37270, Birmingham, New Street 1896

B354050, Bournville, Mary Vale Road 1949

B355017, Brierley Hill, High Street c1965

30914, Coventry, Bishops Street 1892

D103056, Dudley, the Market Place 1957

H365011, Harborne, High Street c1955

S336012, Sedgeley, Bull Ring 1968

S337001, Shirley, Stratford Road c1955

S257093, Solihull, Warwick Road c1965

84685, Stourbridge, High Street 1931

S339006, Sutton Coldfield, the Parade 1949

W161001, Walsall, Bridge 1908

W285005, Wolverhampton, Victoria Street 1910

A143022, AMESBURY, SALISBURY STREET c1950

A80002, AVEBURY, HIGH STREET WEST c1908

51504, BIDDESTONE, THE VILLAGE 1904

B293002, BLUNSDON, COTTAGES 1906

45377, BRADFORD-ON-AVON, MARKET STREET 1900

57208, BURBAGE, VILLAGE 1907

C228053, CALNE, HIGH STREET 1957

57832, CASTLE COMBE, 1907

60955, CHILTON FOLIAT, THE VILLAGE 1908

C294032, CHIPPENHAM, HIGH STREET c1955

51469, CORSHAM, HIGH STREET 1904

44845, DEVIZES, MARKET PLACE 1898

57218, DURLEY, 1907

E163008, EAST KNOYLE, THE VILLAGE c1955

45360, ERLESTOKE, VILLAGE 1900

56377, Harnham, Village 1906

K168007, Kington St Michael, the Village c1960

L1002, Lacock, High Street c1960

76144, Malmesbury, 1924

48637, Marlborough, Town Hall 1902

M166015, Mere, Salisbury Street c1960

42321, Potterne, Old Houses and Church 1898

57196, Ramsbury, High Street 1906

44851, Rowde, Village 1899

80917, Salisbury, Poultry Cross & Silver Street 1928

S254063, Swindon, Regent Street 1961

45344, Trowbridge, Silver Street 1900

W261001, Warminster, the Market Place 1949

68944, Wilton, West Street 1919

W171010, Wootton Bassett, High Street c1955

Yorkshire

45603, AISKEW, THE VILLAGE 1900

A120001, AISLABY, THE VILLAGE c1955

58636, ALDBOROUGH, 1907

A128003, APPLETON-LE-STREET, THE VILLAGE c1960

A129003, APPLETREEWICK, MAIN STREET c1955

A131010, ARMTHORPE, CHURCH STREET c1960

A133013, ASKERN, MOSS ROAD c1965

67231, ASKRIGG, MAIN STREET 1914

A134017, ASTON, THE VILLAGE c1960

60790, AYSGARTH, VILLAGE 1908

B332059, BAILDON, TOWN CENTRE c1965

75706, BAINBRIDGE, THE VILLAGE 1924

B333004, BARNSLEY, MARKET HILL 1948

38279, BEDALE, 1896

79084, BINGLEY, MAIN STREET 1926

B337003, BIRSTALL, MARKET PLACE c1955

61883, BOLTON ABBEY, DEVONSHIRE ARMS HOTEL 1909

58628, BOROUGHBRIDGE, HIGH STREET 1907

54835, BOSTON SPA, HIGH STREET 1906

39509, BRADFORD, MARKET STREET 1897

67217, CARPERBY, VILLAGE AND CROSS 1914

65487, CATTERICK, THE VILLAGE 1913

C262001, CLAYTON WEST, CHURCH STREET c1960

D98008, DENBY DALE, HIGH STREET c1955

49854, DONCASTER, STATION ROAD 1903

E79007, ELLAND, THE CROSS c1965

E82001, EPPLEBY, CROSS KEYS HOTEL c1955

F166009, FERRYBRIDGE, FRONT STREET c1955

39343, FILEY, THE PROMENADE 1897

74322, GOATHLAND, VILLAGE 1923

79060, Grassington, the Square 1926

G112048, Great Ayton, High Street c1965

H9001, Halifax, Town Hall 1900

77862, Hardrow, 1925

71649, Harrogate, Station Square 1921

66037, Hauxwell, 1913

60795, Hawes, 1908

39097, Headingley, Church and Old Oak 1897

H199015, Heckmondwike, Market Place c1960

H201045, Helmsley, the Square c1955

H211003, Hipperholme, High Street c1965

66033, Hipswell, the Village 1913

47133, Horsforth, Town Street 1901

H151020, Huddersfield, New Street 1957

63556, Ilkley, the Grove 1911

79129, INGLETON, INGLEBORO HOTEL 1926

K60011, KEIGHLEY, CAVENDISH STREET c1955

45801, KETTLEWELL, VILLAGE 1900

K72044, KIPPAX, HIGH STREET c1960

K130010, KIRKBYMOORSIDE, c1955

71673, KNARESBOROUGH, VIADUCTS AND BOATING 1921

34766, LEEDS, TOWN HALL 1894

21690, LEYBURN, MARKET PLACE 1889

L168017, LONG PRESTON, MAIN ROAD c1955

L169019, LOW ROW, POST OFFICE AND CHURCH c1955

M139024, MALHAM, THE VILLAGE c1955

M141018, MALTON, MARKET PLACE 1959

60706, MASHAM, SILVER STREET 1908

79035, MIDDLEHAM, MARKET PLACE 1926

M146013, MILNSBRIDGE, MARKET STREET c1955

M149014, MORLEY, QUEENS STREET C1965

A126015, NORTH ANSTON, HIGH STREET C1960

N75001, NORTHALLERTON, HIGH STREET C1955

O49003, OTLEY, KIRKGATE 1953

P154004, PENISTONE, HIGH STREET C1960

P155023, PONTEFRACT, BEASTFAIR C1965

63450, PRESTON-UNDER-SCAR, 1911

Q15002, QUEENSBURY, HIGH STREET C1965

59492, RICHMOND, MARKET PLACE 1908

47179, RIPON, MARKET PLACE 1901

R41052, ROBIN HOOD'S BAY, BAY HOTEL C1965

R60039, ROTHERHAM, TOWN CENTRE C1965

R248001, ROYSTON, POST OFFICE & MIDLAND ROAD C1955

61871, SALTAIRE, STATION 1909

28818, SCARBOROUGH, WESTBORO' 1891

68169, Selby, Market Cross 1918

31962, Sheffield, Crimean Monument 1893

61865, Shipley, 1909

45756, Skipton, High Street 1900

S310004, Slaithwaite, the Village c1960

18209, Staithes, 1886

58625, Tadcaster, Bridge Street 1907

T306030, Thirsk, Market Day c1955

T303038, Thorne, Market Place c1965

T139060, Thornton Dale, the Forge c1955

T136002, Tickhill, Market Place c1955

W464001, Wakefield, Cross Square c1955

61731, Wetherby, North Street 1909

66266, Whitby, the Bridge 1913

61723, York, Coney Street 1909

B269001, Ballymoney, High Street c1900

40187A, Belfast, Donegall Place 1897

40282, Carrickfergus, 1898

C219003, Cork, Patricks Street c1900

40286, Donaghadee, Wharf 1897

D76002, Downpatrick, Irish Street 1900

39210, Dublin, Trinity College and Bank 1897

40684, Glengarriff, Eccles Hotel 1897

H409006, Hillsborough, Castle Street 1890

39296, Howth, the Front 1897

40647, Killarney, 'Meeting of the Waters' 1897

39308, Kingstown, Harbour 1897

L142001, Larne, Main Street c1890

L138001, Lisburn, Market Square 1896

40406, Portrush, Main Street 1897

Scotland

A92001, ABBOTSFORD, FROM THE TWEED 1890

A90002, ABERDEEN, MARKET CROSS 1892

45910, ABERDOUR, HIGH STREET 1900

39858, ALLOWAY, BURNS' COTTAGE 1897

A93001, ARRAN, CASTLE AND LOCH RANZA c1890

A60005, ARROCHAR, THE SHORE FROM LOCH LONG c1955

46002, AYR, HIGH STREET 1900

B267001, BEN NEVIS, FROM CORPACH 1890

B266002, BRAEMAR, MILL ON THE CLUNIE 1890

44675, BRIDGE OF ALLAN, 1899

44634, CALLANDER, MAIN STREET 1899

C208004, CLYDEBANK, GLASGOW ROAD 1900

C359005, COLDSTREAM, HIGH STREET c1955

52676, COMRIE, DRUMMOND STREET 1904

43926, CRIEFF, HIGH STREET 1899

D130306, DALRYMPLE, MAIN STREET c1955

44389, DRUMTOCHTY, VILLAGE 1899

39809, DUMBARTON, 1897

D78002, DUMFRIES, OLD AND NEW BRIDGES c1890

44652, DUNBLANE, CATHEDRAL FROM THE RIVER 1899

D81001, DUNDEE, ALEXANDRA FOUNTAIN 1907

52620, DUNOON, THE PIER 1904

39121, EDINBURGH, CASTLE FROM GRASSMARKET 1897

E56004, ELGIN, 1890

39141, FORTH BRIDGE, 1897

F63002, FRASERBURGH, HERRING BOATS c1900

47492, GARELOCHHEAD, FROM THE PIER 1901

44393, GILMERTON, VILLAGE 1899

39759, GLASGOW, GEORGE SQUARE 1897

43199, GLENCOE, 1899

G81001, GLENCOE, THE SCENE OF THE MASSACRE 1890

45978, GOUROCK, KEMPOCK STREET 1900

39814, GREENOCK, CUSTOMS HOUSE QUAY 1897

H248001, HAWICK, HIGH STREET 1952

47404, HELENSBURGH, PRINCES STREET 1901

39168, HOLYROOD PALACE, ARTHUR'S SEAT 1897

45921, INCHCOLM, 1900

43201, INVERARAY, 1899

I25003, INVERNESS, FROM THE CASTLE c1890

50887, IONA, 1903

53154, IRVINE, THE HARBOUR 1904

K55001, KELSO, c1890

K51001, KILLIN, c1890

44636, KILMAHOG, VILLAGE 1899

39833, KIRN, 1897

K50002, KIRRIEMUIR, HIGH STREET C1890

39847, KYLES OF BUTE, 1897

39856, LARGS, 1897

39157, LINLITHGOW, 1897

44419, LOCH EARN, 1899

47498, LOCH GOIL, AND LOCH LONG 1901

44590, LOCH KATRINE, 1899

L94001, LOCH LOMOND, THE ISLAND FROM LUSS C1890

47503, LOCH LONG, HIGHLAND CATTLE 1901

47438, MELROSE, THE SQUARE 1901

39857, MILLPORT, 1897

M113002, MOFFAT, HIGH STREET 1890

M179037, MORRISTON, THE CROSS 1954

44380, MUTHILL, 1899

39139, NEWHAVEN, HARBOUR 1897

39176, North Berwick, Quality Street 1897

47511, Oban, George Street 1901

47397, Paisley, Dunn Square 1901

43900, Perth, High Street West 1899

P125001, Portree, Skye 1890

39824, River Clyde, Yachts on the Clyde 1897

39836, Rothesay, Pier 1897

43914, Scone Palace, north west 1899

44396, Sma Glen, 1899

52944, St Fillans, 1904

50897, Staffa, Fingal's Cave 1903

45928, Stanley, Percy Street 1900

44705, Stirling, Broad Street 1899

44620, Strathyre, Village 1899

T102001, Tarbert, Loch Fyne 1890

A182050, ABERAERON, MAIN STREET C1955

46974, ABERDOVEY, THE QUAY 1901

41675, ABERGAVENNY, CROSS STREET 1898

36573, ABERGELE, 1895

47010, ABERSOCH, CONGREGATIONAL CHURCH 1901

A195024, ABERTRIDWR, THE SQUARE C1965

44526, ABERYSTWYTH, BEACH 1899

A297006, ALLTWEN, HEOL Y PARC C1965

A186019, AMMANFORD, COLLEGE STREET C1955

37706, BALA, HIGH STREET 1896

60732, BANGOR, HIGH STREET 1908

B300013, BARGOED, HIGH STREET C1955

60216, BARMOUTH, HIGH STREET 1908

50852, BARRY, HOLTON ROAD 1903

62564, BARRY ISLAND, 1910

Wales

63301, BEAUMARIS, CHURCH STREET 1911

77847, BEDDGELERT, 1925

B475016, BEDWAS, CHURCH STREET C1965

83619, BETHESDA, THE VILLAGE 1930

32750, BISHOPSTON, 1893

B658006, BLACKWOOD, HIGH STREET C1960

46741, BLAENAU FFESTINIOG, CHURCH STREET 1901

44535, BORTH, PARADE AND BEACH 1899

62648, BRECON, THE BULWARK 1910

41199, BRIDGEND, 1898

B396119, BUILTH WELLS, HIGH STREET C1955

54826, CAERNARVON, SQUARE 1906

43623, CAERPHILLY, CASTLE STREET 1899

29537, CAPEL CURIG, 1891

32678, CARDIFF, QUEEN STREET 1893

27992, Carew Castle, Bridge 1890

77283, Carmarthen, Guildhall Square 1925

C553043, Carno, Main Street c1965

47964, Caswell Bay, 1901

C365011, Cefn Mawr, Well Street c1955

54507, Chepstow, High Street 1906

88007, Cheriton, 1937

C340003, Clydach, High Street and Hospital c1965

46268, Colwyn Bay, Pier Pavilion 1900

29450A, Conway, the Castle 1891

C313083, Cowbridge, High Street c1955

41694, Crickhowell, 1898

32646, Crumlin, Viaduct 1893

20848, Denbigh, Market Place 1888

83598, Dolgellau, Market Square 1930

88363, Duffryn, Afan Road 1938

E176014, Ebbw Vale, Bethcar Street c1960

36295, Erddig, 1895

65902, Fairbourne, Parade 1913

43641, Fishguard, 1899

F120036, Flint, High Street c1965

G149047, Glyn Neath, High Street c1955

87814, Gorseinon, the Square 1936

G152003, Gowerton, Sterry Road c1955

G153006, Gwaun-cae-Gurwen, Carmel Street c1955

21737, Harlech, Castle 1889

53751, Haverfordwest, Mariners Square 1906

49656, Hawarden, Village 1903

H392024, Hay-on-Wye, Broad Street c1955

H288007, Henllan, Henllan Falls Hotel c1955

30299, HOLYHEAD, SOUTH STACK LIGHTHOUSE 1892

K92005, KENFIG, THE SQUARE 1966

K144006, KERRY, HIGH STREET C1955

77315, KIDWELLY, STATION ROAD 1925

K61106, KNIGHTON, HIGH STREET C1955

L204015, LAMPETER, HARFORD SQUARE 1931

27986, LAMPHEY, CHURCH AND VILLAGE 1890

32744, LANGLANDS BAY, THE HOTEL 1893

L145105, LLANDRINDOD WELLS, GLEN USK HOTEL C1955

60754, LLANDUDNO, PARADE 1908

38736, LLANELLY, STEPNEY STREET 1896

60771, LLANFAIRFECHAN, MAIN STREET 1908

L364074, LLANGEFNI, MARKET C1960

88004, LLANMADOG, CWM IVY 1937

88275, LLANSAMLET, HEOL LAS 1938

32612, LLANTHONY, VALLEY 1895

46963, MACHYNLLETH, MAENGWYN STREET 1901

27981, MANORBIER, CASTLE 1890

23187, MENAI, BRIDGE 1890

M118005, MERTHYR TYDFIL, PONT-MOLARIS c1955

M77038, MILFORD HAVEN, CHARLES STREET c1955

M201036, MOLD, THE CROSS c1955

28784, MONMOUTH, 1891

M175021, MOUNTAIN ASH, OXFORD STREET 1950

77405, MUMBLES, SOUTH END 1925

N115022, NARBERTH, HIGH STREET c1955

N5030, NEATH, ST DAVID'S CHURCH c1965

N64025, NEWGALE, THE OLD WELSH ROAD 1954

47896, NEWPORT, COMMERCIAL STREET 1901

N171108, NEWTOWN, c1965

54796, Old Colwyn, 1906

62598, Oxwich, the Castle 1910

32756, Parkmill, the Village 1893

27972, Pembroke, High Street 1890

P203026, Pembroke Dock, from Barrack Hill c1960

P180008, Pen-Clawdd, the Village c1955

38464, Penarth, from the Pier 1896

P205043, Pendine, c1955

P196010, Penley, Village c1955

65677, Penmaenmawr, Parade 1913

65873, Penmaenpool, 1913

87981, Penrice Castle, the Village 1937

P183009, Pontardawe, the Cross c1965

P165016, Pontarddulais, Swansea Road c1965

43614, Pontypridd, Penuel Chapel 1899

P76046, PORT EYNON, THE VILLAGE c1955

P139020, PORT TALBOT, STATION ROAD 1952

88461, PORTHCAWL, JOHN STREET 1938

60728, PORTMADOC, HIGH STREET 1908

36603, PRESTATYN, 1895

30187, PWLLHELI, THE PROMENADE 1892

87735A, PYLE, THE VILLAGE 1936

R294001, RADYR, STATION ROAD c1965

54517, RAGLAN, CASTLE 1906

32526, REDBROOK, 1893

R275011, RESOLVEN, THE CITADEL c1965

70794, RHOS-ON-SEA, 1921

R291023, RHUABON, HIGH STREET c1955

46284, RHYL, PARADE 1900

36307, ROSSETT, THE MILL 1895

Wales

77281, SAUNDERSFOOT, THE HARBOUR 1925

S440007, SENGHENNYDD, CLOCK TOWER c1965

87892, SKEWEN, THE ARCHES 1937

37764, SNOWDON, MOUNTAIN RAILWAY 1896

87658, SOUTHGATE, THE VILLAGE 1936

23293, ST ASAPH, FROM THE BRIDGE 1890

27907, ST DAVIDS, 1890

32716, ST FAGANS, CASTLE AND VILLAGE 1893

38754, SWANSEA, WIND STREET & VIVIAN STATUE 1896

87701, TALGARTH, HIGH STREET 1936

28041, TENBY, THE HARBOUR 1890

76881, TINTERN, 1925

T192008, TONYPANDY, CLYDACH STREET c1955

86876, WAUNFAWR, POST OFFICE 1935

49689, WREXHAM, HOPE STREET 1903